Woman's *Best* Friend

Choosing and Training the Dog That's Right for You

Babette Haggerty-Brennan

Contemporary Books

Chicago   New York   San Francisco   Lisbon   London   Madrid   Mexico City
Milan   New Delhi   San Juan   Seoul   Singapore   Sydney   Toronto

Library of Congress Cataloging-in-Publication Data

Haggerty-Brennan, Babette.
    Woman's best friend : choosing and training the dog that's right for you / Babette
Haggerty-Brennan.
        p.   cm.
    Includes bibliographical references and index.
    ISBN 0-07-141740-0
    1. Dogs.   2. Dogs—Selection.   3. Dogs—Training.   4. Women dog
owners.   I. Title.

SF426.H25   2003
636.7—dc21   2003048587

To the three most wonderful men—
My hero and dad, Captain Haggerty, for teaching me the love of a dog.
My best friend and husband, Gordon Brennan, for teaching me about
true love, devotion, and commitment.
My precious son, Ryan Arthur Brennan, who has given me the gift of love
only a mother can understand.
I am so blessed and grateful God has given me the three of you—I love you!

1 2 3 4 5 6 7 8 9 0   AGM/AGM   2 1 0 9 8 7 6 5 4 3

ISBN 0-07-141740-0

Interior design by Think Design Group

McGraw-Hill books are available at special quantity discounts to use as premiums and sales
promotions, or for use in corporate training programs. For more information, please write to
the Director of Special Sales, Professional Publishing, McGraw-Hill, Two Penn Plaza,
New York, NY 10121-2298. Or contact your local bookstore.

This book is printed on acid-free paper.

Contents

Foreword

When I first met Babette Haggerty-Brennan, I had a precious and precocious three-month-old Golden Retriever puppy. Cali needed a few lessons in doggy etiquette, and Babette was eager and willing to take her on.

Babette has a natural rapport and loving instinct with dogs that they immediately sense. She also knew how to work with Cali so that she would adapt to our personal lifestyle and become a devoted and much-loved member of our family.

Women, obviously, bring pets into their homes for different reasons—companionship, protection, therapy. Or, as Babette says, "Nurturing is the biggest reason women get dogs, as they want to nurture someone in return for their unconditional love."

Dogs come in all different shapes, sizes, and personalities, and the dog that is right for me may not be right for you. Read and take note of Babette's advice in these areas.

Babette has an impeccable reputation in the world of professional dog trainers. She is a full-time wife and mother, which makes her even more sensitive to the needs and concerns of women.

You will enjoy the following pages as Babette shares her personal and professional ideas on how to select, train, and fall in love with that perfect dog. She takes our knowledge of this to a higher level.

Although commonly known as "man's best friend," dogs are, Babette assures us, first and foremost, "woman's best friend."

—Barbara Nicklaus

Preface

Training dogs is different for women than it is for men. Dogs listen better to men. Yet, we are better trainers than men.

We are patient, nurturing, and more generous with praise. We understand that before you run, you need to walk. Men often just want the dog to get a beer out of the refrigerator. Women understand that we first need to give our dog a foundation of obedience skills and basic manners before we would teach her that.

Why Did I Write This Book?

There is nothing better than being a woman. However, women are overworked and underpaid. We have careers, children, lovers, spouses, housework, and we also take care of the dog. Men could never do all that we do.

We need to simplify our lives. There are many ways to train dogs, but the training needs to be easy and realistic. I am going to teach you how to train and manage your girl better.

My training began with my dad, Captain Haggerty, who has become internationally recognized as a pioneer in dog training. My dad started teaching me how to teach tricks and obedience in 1974. He always said that I needed to give bigger treats to the dogs.

I have put my own spin on dog training. Training for me is ever evolving, and it is always different based on the dog and the owner's needs and abilities. Like my dad, I keep many tools in my training toolbox. I will use all of them for the right dog and owner. My dad has trained tens of thousands of dogs, and he has personally trained more than one hundred professional trainers. His legacy is untouchable. Countless people over the years have told me how he has inspired them as trainers.

On vacation my husband and I visited a well-known dog behaviorist. While we were sitting in his mountaintop home in Berkeley, California, he said to me, "I knew that I made it when your dad showed up at one of my seminars."

I began training dogs professionally while in college. It snowballed from there, and I founded Babette Haggerty's School for Dogs in Palm Beach Gardens, Florida. Our school's reputation has grown beyond my wildest dreams. Proven by our alumni referrals, we are known for quality training, value, and satisfied customers. I also get to go home to Manhattan twice a month to train clients' dogs.

What This Book Is

Obedience training helps set the foundation for the rules by which we want our dogs to live; it gives them a job to do and calms them. Indirectly, it helps stop a lot of problems from developing.

If you want your dog to stop a bad behavior today, not in years, then you will immensely enjoy this book. It is filled with tried-and-true tricks for you to have a well-trained, happy dog. This book is about teaching your dog what to do and what not to do.

It is important to provide leadership and positive discipline for dogs. I don't mean you should bully your dog—you wouldn't bully a child—but you want to train and encourage good behavior.

Our dogs want to please us, but most often they just do not know how. Imagine going to Zimbabwe, not knowing the language and having to live with a family and fit into their lifestyle. There is no one to translate for you. That is what happens to our dogs: we put them in our environment and expect them to understand the rules even though we haven't even explained them.

This book is filled with true tales and some embarrassing moments. We will talk about forbidden topics such as sex, dogs, and rock and roll. I believe that I have taken a sometimes-dry topic—dog training—and made it fun and entertaining.

What This Book Isn't

If you want political correctness, this book is not for you. In the last ten years, it has become politically incorrect to correct your dog. A vociferous few will state that you should teach a dog what you want and ignore the bad behavior.

Unfortunately, some dogs have been deemed hopeless and sentenced to death because these totally positive trainers don't want to correct them. Correction-free training has had this problem since its inception.

I speak both from my experience and research into my collection of dog books, some dating as far back as 1848. People have been training dogs by showing them what to do, praising good behavior, and stopping bad behavior for centuries. This was happening long before Skinner proved that if you give the rat cheese he will repeat the behavior and if you zap him he will stop.

Yes, I could be politically correct and defraud you, but you wouldn't get the results you need. In my opinion, you and your dog deserve a complete training program with a high standard of training rather than incomplete training with lower standards.

The Art of Praise

I praise loudly. I blame softly.

—*Catherine II of Russia, 1729–1796*

Praise is so important. Praise and reward must be constant and consistent. You cannot overpraise your dog. Different types of praise affect dogs differently.

We are going to use the five senses to praise our dogs. We use sound when we speak in a happy voice. Touch will include different types of rubbing and massage and lots of loving hugs. When you want your dog to relax and stay calm, as in a down-stay, you will stroke her lightly and softly. We use sight when we smile at her with approval. And we will engage her senses of smell and taste with treats.

When you are using treats, keep in mind the concept of diminishing marginal returns. You may recognize this term from Economics 101. The example my professor used to illustrate this concept was how on a hot day an ice-cold Coca-Cola tastes great, but a second one isn't as good as the first. The same thing happens with treats. After that first treat, subsequent treats are not as pleasing to your dog. As soon as your dog starts responding to treats, you need to start weaning her from them.

To Correct or Not to Correct— That Is the Question

Don't compromise yourself. You are all you've got.

—Janis Joplin

If your dog never does anything wrong, you will never have to stop her misbehavior. That would be terrific! However, you probably wouldn't read this book if that were the case.

Corrections are something that stops a dog's bad behavior and when timed correctly, stops the dog from thinking about it. If you give your dog a correction and it doesn't stop the behavior, it is not a correction.

There are many kinds of corrections including a verbal "no" in a deep voice, squinty eyes giving a stern look, taking away a treat or a toy, stopping the petting, a startling sound, a leash correction, or a spray of water.

The correction must fit your dog's personality and the crime. You are going to use a warning voice or look when your dog is thinking about breaking a sit-stay, but you are going to use a much stronger correction if she growls at you for going near her food bowl.

There should never be any hitting, yelling, screaming, smacking, scruffing, rolling, growling, or shaking. If you find yourself becoming angry and frustrated, walk away. Give yourself time to cool down.

Like praise, corrections must be consistent. If you are finding yourself correcting over and over again for the same thing, then reassess what you are doing. Chances are what you think is a correction your dog does not perceive as one. Corrections must be fair and clear. When in doubt, get help.

Remember that ignoring bad behavior takes the longest to modify. If you wait to let the behavior extinguish itself, it can take forever. Dogs need to have clear-cut instructions on what we want and don't want. If you ignore bad behavior, it will take a long time for your dog to figure out why you aren't happy and you will both be miserable. Ignoring bad behavior accomplishes nothing and is simply unfair. Dogs don't read our minds. Be fair and tell her what you want.

The C Word

Now, if this were a book for the other sex, they would run away. However, we are smarter and more courageous; therefore, the C word does not scare us. It stands for *consistent*:

- consistent encouragement
- consistent practice
- consistent reward
- consistent correction
- consistent patience

If you only praise good behavior some of the time, your dog will only do it less than some of the time. If you correct bad behavior some of the time, she knows that sometimes she can get away with it. Such inconsistency is called slot-machine training and will cause your dog to think along these lines: sometimes I win, sometimes I lose. I never know when I will win or lose so I will just keep trying to get away with the bad behavior.

To Get the Most Out of This Book

Before you start training your dog, take her to your vet for a complete physical. This will reveal any hidden symptoms of physical trouble that could lead to behavioral problems.

Next, write specific goals, such as "I want my dog to stop pulling on her leash." After each session, write an evaluation, such as, "My timing is improving," or "I need to talk more to my dog."

Before you begin training your dog a new command, make sure to perform the visualization and positive affirmation exercises in this book. They will help you get into a proper mind-set for training. As you train your dog, don't skip steps or commands. Sometimes I outline various approaches to teaching a command. Using the approach that is easiest for you, practice each new command for three to five days before moving on to the next command.

There are many stories in this book—some funny, some bizarre, and some touching. They are all true, but please know that in order to protect the privacy of my clients, I have changed their and their dogs' names as well as other descriptive traits.

The journey upon which you are about to embark, I hope, will be enlightening and enjoyable. It is my wish that your best friend will be better than you ever dreamed.

I thank you for choosing my book. Like lovers, there are so many books and so little time. If you have questions, during your training, please feel free to E-mail me at Babette@HaggertyDog .com and place *Woman's Best Friend* in the subject line.

ACKNOWLEDGMENTS

There are so many to thank who gave me time, info, and support for this book: Many of my dad's former students and employees and colleagues who have not only encouraged me along the way to carry on the Haggerty family dog training tradition but have also taken me under their wings and have shared their knowledge with me. Joyce and Arvind DeBraganca, Martin and Pat Deeley, Steve Diller, Liz Doup, Jennifer Jolley, Bob Maida, and Sarah Piumbroeck. Gary Wilkes for straightening out misinformation on clicker training. Liz Mayer for contributing her photographic talents. Bill Dillard for giving me so much history on lost information. Lois Meistrell, Edi Munneke of Rusticana Kennels, Catharine Reiley, Ursula Roper and the Poodle Obedience Training Club of Greater New York, Christa Skiebe, Wynn Strickland, Kate Weiner, and the Seeing Eye. My very cool cousin, John Urcioli, for pointing me in the right direction and being like a brother to me. Dr. Mike Berkenblit and the staff at Village Animal Clinic in North Palm Beach, Florida, for always being so good to me. Dr. Ochstein and the staff at Island Animal Hospital in Palm Beach, Florida. My dad for nudging me for years to write a book. Carol Benjamin for cheering me on. My agent, Noah Lukeman of Lukeman Literary Agency. Michele Pezzuti—a tremendous editor and a very cool Jersey girl. You really believed in this book and thank you. Heidi Bresnahan, a great editor, who made it all so easy. The Dog Writers List. My first English professor, Melinda Goodman, who told me to keep writing. Carlos and Sandy Mejias of Olde Towne School for Dogs, Alexandria, Virginia. Michael Brogan for giving me insight. Mrs. Barbara Nicklaus for being an excellent example for all women to follow: a supportive wife, a loving mother, a smart businesswoman, and a true lady. Mike Camardello, Mark Frankel, and Pet Supplies Plus of North Palm Beach and Delray Beach, Florida. Jill Hendelman. Michele Mayo from Ocean Massage Therapy. Caroline Thurber for telling me that I needed to write a book. Chuck and Donna Schooley of Schooley Cadillac of West Palm Beach, Florida. A. J. Morton and his wonderful assistant Helen Freshour for the vibrant photography. Susan King and Ana Parker for all their help. Jacquie Blomquist. Ashley and Alexa Young—two wonderful girls—and their mom and my great friend, Becky. The "Hooligans" for comic relief and friendship. My Aunt Mary for helping in so many ways. My most wonderful husband, Gordon, for being very patient with me. You have been a tremendous support. Our little blessing Ryan Arthur. We love you tremendously. My students and owners who have each taught me something. All of the dogs and their owners who allowed me to photograph them in the heat of August in South Florida, especially the Donlens, the Douglasses, Johnny and Colleen Hernandez, the Kinos, the Levins, the Sterns, the Rodmans, and the Van de Waters.

Introduction

The History of Women in Dog Training

*We must remember that one
determined person can make a
significant difference, and that a small
group of determined people can
change the course of history.*

—*Sonia Johnson*

Men always take the credit for the work we women achieve. Hey, we know the truth, so what difference does it make? Many men have trained and worked their dogs in the field for hunting and herding from the beginning of their partnership with woman's best friend. However, it was women who actually started dog training, as we know it today.

A native of Philadelphia, Dorothy Eustis lived in Switzerland for eight years training German Shepherd Dogs for the Red Cross, as well as for the Swiss army and police. In 1927 she wrote an article for the *Saturday Evening Post* about the Blind Institute in Potsdam, Germany, which trained dogs for guide dog work for World War I veterans. Many people wrote her asking for help in finding a guide dog in the United States. Once she realized that there was such a need in the States, she began the Seeing Eye in 1929. Originally founded in Nashville, Tennessee, the school moved to Morristown, New Jersey, where it still provides the training of guide dogs.

Dorothy Harrison Eustis. Photo courtesy of the Seeing Eye.

Helene Whitehouse Walker was a socialite and a dog lover. She raised and showed Standard Poodles. Mrs. Whitehouse Walker grew tired of everyone believing that her Standard Poodles were only balls of beautiful fluff. She decided to prove the naysayers wrong—her dogs were like all women—beautiful and brainy. She learned about obedience firsthand on a trip to England. She inspired the first competitive obedience test in the United States in 1933. Held in Mount Kisco, New York, on her father's estate, the obedience test began public interest in obedience training. She approached the American Kennel Club with competition information. The American Kennel Club, both thrilled and intrigued by what she was sharing, asked her to educate people in obedience.

In 1934 Mrs. Whitehouse Walker enlisted Blanche Saunders for help. Ms. Saunders had worked for her, caring, handling, conditioning, and showing her Poodles. They packed up a motor home and traveled to all the big cities throughout the country. By the time the United States began its involvement in World War II, Saunders and Walker had covered the entire country. They educated people about training and competition. Dog owners hadn't realized they could train their own dogs. Thanks to Mrs. Whitehouse Walker and Ms. Saunders, owners today know they can train their dogs. It is undeniable that they are the first ladies of obedience.

Between 1940 and 1945 dogs received large amounts of publicity. Many families donated their dogs to the war effort. With the affluence the United States experienced after World War II, the number of families with dogs as pets grew. The purebred dog became the latest status symbol. The sharing of one's life with a dog, along with the education efforts of Blanche Saunders and Helene Whitehouse Walker, created a need for dog-training professionals.

During the 1940s through the 1970s the late Bea Godsol was known as a great mentor and judge. She was one of the early women pioneers in dog training, conducting training clinics and classes at her ranch in California. Later, both she and her husband, Colonel Major Godsol, judged and trained throughout the world.

Mrs. Helene Whitehouse Walker with Glee of Carillon Epreuve UDT and Tango of Piperscroft CDX.
Photo courtesy of Ursula Roper and the Poodle Obedience Training Club of Greater New York.

Edi Munneke worked as a schoolteacher for more than thirty years. After school she trained dogs for basic manners and competed in obedience trials, first with Wirehaired Fox Terriers and then later with Golden Retrievers. In the 1950s, most of the better-

Blanche Saunders doing what she loved and did best—training dogs!
Photo courtesy of Ursula Roper and the Poodle Obedience Training Club of Greater New York.

Walker and Saunders traveled cross-country in this trailer—an unbelievable feat for two fearless women in the 1930s.

Photo courtesy of Ursula Roper and the Poodle Obedience Training Club of Greater New York.

known trainers were men who had returned from the war; however, the larger percentage of trainers comprised women. The women teaching the group classes were mostly housewives and thought of training as a hobby, something that gave them an opportunity to get out of the house. Most did it as volunteer work for their local obedience clubs. As obedience clubs began to spring up all over the country at this time, the classes were designed for obedience competition rather than for developing a problem-free dog.

Lois Meistrell owned and operated Great Neck Dog Training Center. Mrs. Meistrell was a pioneer in field trials and obedience competition. When speaking of her experiences, Mrs. Meistrell, a Vermont resident, now in her mid-nineties, will claim that her husband, Harland, was the better of the duo. Old-timers in the dog world strongly disagree. Working and training all breeds, she was on television for more than thirty-two weeks, showing children how to work with dogs. The Meistrells were training from the 1940s through the 1960s. What is so interesting about this particular era was that the Meistrells were conducting group obedience classes in the ballrooms of New York City hotels on a weekly basis. This would be unheard of today. Lois and Harland referred to themselves as *cynologists*, not trainers, a term that simply means "students of dog behavior." She will let anyone know that she can't thank Blanche Saunders or Helene Whitehouse Walker enough for their role in establishing obedience training and competition.

A great contributor to obedience and an even greater one to German Shepherd Dogs is undoubtedly Winifred Strickland. At the 1965 national German Shepherd Dog specialty in Phoenix, Arizona, Winifred Strickland amazed the audience with her "agility" test, putting her dog Joll through a series of obstacles and jumps. Many people in the audience hadn't realized how much their dogs could learn. This was at least ten years before a simpler version of agility came to this country. Not only known for earning many first places in competition, Ms. Strickland also wrote the first book for dog-training instructors and was the first to make obedience-training videos. In 2000 she was recognized by the AKC for having more than two hundred obedience titles. This is a first in obedience, and the titles were all on her own dogs. To mention all of Ms. Strickland's accomplishments and contributions to dog obedience and the German Shepherd Dog would be a book in itself. Also in 2000, the German Shepherd Dog Club of America dedicated its National Specialty Show to her. She has given over fifty years of selfless and tireless devotion to the breed.

Blanche Saunders in later years.
Photo courtesy of Ursula Roper and the Poodle Obedience Training Club of Greater New York.

Anyone who knows Wynn, as she is affectionately called, knows her to be a lady who brings an outstanding amount of integrity to the sport with a willingness to help the new person.

My parents always told me to never ask my elders their age. I am not sure how old Ms. Strickland is but this petite woman is still actively competing, writing books, breeding dogs, and training German Shepherds when many women her age and size would have scaled down to a Toy Poodle.

The most entertaining woman who brought dog training to your living room was a white-haired, stern woman named Barbara Woodhouse. Uttering the command "walkies" spoken in a British shrill, she brought laughter and enjoyment to anyone who watched her. Formerly a horse trainer, she rose quickly to dog fame with her television show "Dog Training by Barbara Woodhouse." Dressed in a wool sweater and plaid kilt, she was a much bigger hit than the BBC had expected. She had a firm approach to training owners and their dogs. Strongly convicted in her beliefs, she received criticism and still does. Agree or disagree with her techniques, no one can fairly deny that dogs responded to her ways. With the large attendance

Wynthea's Joll v Summerland, UDT, jumps through a sixteen-inch hoop in perfect form at a height of four feet assisted by trainer Winifred Strickland.

Photo provided by Winifred Strickland, Wynthea Kennels.

she drew to her two-day obedience course and her television show, she helped save the lives of thousands of dogs.

There have been many more women who have made great contributions to the evolving world of dogs, whether it be in training, showing, breeding, grooming, writing, or veterinary medicine. There is much yet to be learned, and I believe women will be the ones to carry dogs to a higher plane so that men will finally concede and admit what we have always known: dogs truly are woman's best friend.

CHOOSING A DOG
THAT'S RIGHT FOR YOU

We're Goin' on a Pooch Hunt

Let us love dogs; let us love only dogs!

Men and cats are unworthy creatures.

—Maria Bashkirtseff

All right, so we are going on a dog hunt, which is different than a mate hunt. When searching for mates we worry about our figures, hair, and makeup. Then we have to figure out a respectable way to attract them so that they don't feel hunted. Dogs are different—they don't care about us being fat or having a bad hair day. Nor do we have to worry that we are giving them too much love and affection. We don't have to follow "the Rules." The dogs just need to follow our rules, most of the time.

Why Do I Want a Dog?

There are many different things to consider before deciding on a dog. Ask yourself the following questions:

1. Why do I want a dog? Do I want a friend? A protector?
2. Do I want a purebred? Do I want an all-American mixed breed?

3. What kind of personality do I want? A couch potato? An outgoing social butterfly?
4. Do I want to purchase or adopt?
5. What age of dog do I want?
6. What sex of dog do I want?

A man will often pick the kind of dog he had as a kid. He will claim the dog would follow him to school and wait until he was done to walk him home, knew 168 different commands, and understood four languages, including Mandarin. Men will also tell you that they got their dogs because they were "chick magnets"; whether this was something they read about in *GQ* or not, I am not certain, but dogs are indeed "chick magnets" and guys love that.

Women, on the other hand, get dogs for emotional reasons—for nurturing, for protection, for companionship, for therapy. "My friend found the dog so I took her home." "I want the kids to learn how to take care of a dog." "I went into the pet shop just to look and there she was—she had been there for so long. I couldn't leave her there."

Nurturing is the biggest reason women get dogs; they want a dog to care for in return for unconditional love. Perhaps they have unsuccessfully struggled to have a child; they get a dog and treat her like a surrogate child. I had one client who did just that.

Anna and her husband spent tens of thousands of dollars going to the best doctors with the hopes of getting pregnant. Her husband bought her a beautiful Smooth Fox Terrier. As soon as they got her and started obedience classes, Anna got pregnant. It was wonderful! The dog loves the baby and follows the baby around—they are best friends.

Protection is another big reason single and married women alike get dogs. This is true of many of my clients. Gina hired me to help her with her German Shepherd. She had adopted Jaeger from the shelter because there had been a rapist breaking into people's homes in her suburban neighborhood. Steve and Rachel got Rocky, a male Weimaraner, for protection because Steve was going to be living out of the area for a couple of years. While she was in law school, Lara adopted Chelsea, a thirty-pound all-American dog, because there had been a lot of break-ins in her building. Chelsea stopped the intruder one night from breaking in while Lara was sleeping.

Sometimes problems arise when a man wants a dog to protect his family. He often gets a dog that is too tough.

CASE IN POINT

I remember a gentleman who called wanting a Belgian Malinois to protect his family. He lived on the water in Palm Beach. He had already purchased two protection-trained German Shepherds for an outrageous sum of money and got really ripped off. The dogs were not of good quality and were returned to the seller. So now he had decided on a Belgian Malinois, having been told that it was a better protection dog. Despite my advice, he purchased a very hardy dog. He ended up getting rid of that dog because the dog was too much for his wife and three small children to handle effectively. What is that saying about a fool and his money?

Companionship is another big reason women get dogs. Perhaps they live alone or have just moved to a new town and want a little company. I have many clients who have found true companionship in their dogs. John and Lisa are a nice couple living in Boca Raton, Florida. Lisa had just left her life and career in New York City to marry John. He bought her an adorable Maltese because he knew that getting married and moving to a new place was an adjustment. John didn't want Lisa to be lonely. Another client purchased her Chocolate Labrador Retriever, Cocoa, after she got a divorce. She said, "At least Cocoa isn't going to treat me the way he did."

Women also get dogs for therapy. I worked with a very nice woman in her early thirties who had gotten a Pug. The Pug was quite a handful, yet the woman was determined to work out all of the Pug's problems. She confided in me one day with tears in her eyes: "I got her because I used to have a son, but he died. I can't replace him but . . ." She never finished her sentence. I knew what she was saying. I, too, fought back tears, never wishing that on my worst enemy.

Randy and Stacy purchased a Golden Retriever for therapy. They had been in the process of adopting a child. After months of expecting the child, they arrived at the hospital only to find that the birth mother had changed her mind. They were devastated. They agreed to get a wonderful dog to help heal the pain. The good news is that they were able to adopt another child, and now the Golden is that baby's best friend.

Many women will get a dog "for the kids." They rationalize that getting a dog will give the children responsibility because they will take care of the dog.

CASE IN POINT

A woman recently called me. I returned her call before the end of the day and she said, "Oh, I solved the problem. I am getting rid of the dog. I bought the dog for my son and he isn't taking care of it, so the dog is going." I asked her how old her son was, and when she replied, "eight," I wanted to say, "Lady, your son can't take care of himself. He is eight years old. How do you expect him to take care of a dog?" I refrained and commented, "Yes, eight is young to take care of a dog." She then asked me at what age he should get a dog. I replied, "When he is old enough to pick out the dog, pay for the dog, take care of the dog, and no longer lives at home."

It is unfair to expect a child to take care of a dog. Yes, when they are a little older they are capable of helping with the dog, but they should not be the sole caregiver. Moreover, by the time they are fourteen their friends are probably a lot more important than the family pet, so they won't be around to help as much. And once they turn eighteen, many will move out of the house and leave the dog behind for someone else to take care of. As a rule of thumb, if you get a dog for your children, make sure you are ready to assume full responsibility for the next fifteen years.

There are many dogs that I would recommend for a woman. There are great breeds for protection, nurturing, and companionship. Keep in mind that as a woman, you are more likely to have a change in your lifestyle than a man. Perhaps you will find a life partner. Perhaps you will find yourself a single woman again having survived a divorce or the loss of your spouse. Perhaps your children will leave home and you will become an empty nester. Perhaps you will start a new career or begin taking care of the family full-time.

If you have children or are planning on children, thoroughly investigate adding a dog to your family. I believe your life will be easier if you wait until your last child is at least seven. If you already have a dog and younger children, you shouldn't get rid of your dog. Just be cautious, not only for your child but for your dog as well. There are higher incidences of children hurting dogs than dogs hurting children. This goes unnoticed because when a child hurts a dog, it is a poke in the eye, a pull on the tail, or a hit on the face. The dog will cry in pain, get up, and hide somewhere; the parents don't notice and there isn't a serious enough injury warranting veterinary attention. However, there is evidence when a dog hurts a child; the dog may bite the child or knock the child down, and the child may hit his or her head and need medical attention. Always teach children to play gently with dogs and never to tease them. Stress that they must never disturb dogs when eating or sleeping either.

Dogs can also attract potential friends and lovers. I have a friend, Chris, who lost his sight at seventeen. Chris's mom told me how Chris's whole world changed when he got Chevy, his Yellow Labrador Retriever. People started talking to him. After all, that is how I met Chris. We were in college and I first noticed Chevy. I recognized the name of the guide dog school on Chevy's harness—the Guide Dogs for the Blind. Having visited the school on my honeymoon, I started talking to Chris about it. We became fast friends. We still talk and whenever I am in Orlando, I visit Chris and Chevy.

When I was in college and lived alone, I had a Yorkshire Terrier named Tia and my all-American dog, Soupie, from the shelter that,

POP QUIZ TIME!

What do you do when you see a guide dog and his partner: (1) run up and pet the dog—after all he is so pretty and sweet; (2) give him a cookie; or (3) make friends with the human partner? If you answered 3, you are correct. Remember that guide dogs are working dogs and they are not to be touched or fed by a well-meaning person. You don't have to start talking to the person, but it is always nice to make friends. After all, strangers are just friends we have not met yet.

VERY COOL LOVE STORY

My friend Lara called me when she started dating the man who became her husband. Lara has two dogs and treats them like her children. When my husband and I met her new boyfriend, we thought he was a really nice guy. Our like-him barometer hit the jackpot level when he told us about his two dogs and how they were his pride and joy. Then he told us the story of how the year before his vet had told him his dog was going to die in the next couple of days and that he should consider euthanizing her. Devastated by the news, he put her in the car and drove for three hours before he realized he was on the other coast of Florida. He talked to her the entire time. He turned and asked her if she was ready to go to heaven, and she jumped up and told him no way! That was two years ago and she is still kicking! When he told us that story we knew that he was the one for Lara. Three months later they eloped to Alaska, were married by a dog musher at the top of a glacier, and ended up bringing home a genuine Alaskan Husky as their wedding present. The Alaskan Husky got along famously with their dogs, and so they officially had "your kids," "my kids," and "our kids."

bless his little heart, is still with me. I have had him longer than my husband. Actually, an ex-boyfriend adopted him. I got rid of the boyfriend and kept his dog. Well, the dog did like me better. The ex-boyfriend didn't understand why. After all, I fed, walked, and trained the dog. I can't imagine why, can you? After I got rid of the boyfriend, I started dating other guys. If I thought I wanted to go out with the guy again, I would introduce him to my dogs. Tia especially either loved men or hated them. If both of my dogs liked the guy, I would go out with him again; if they didn't like him, I didn't go out with him again. They were great barometers of suitable men. They loved my husband.

Dogs aren't necessarily only mate barometers; they can be friend barometers as well. I once heard someone say, "Don't trust anyone who doesn't like dogs." I had a friend in college whose dog hated her roommate. I told her to listen to her dog, but she needed a roommate. One day she came home and her roommate had stolen her jewelry, records (remember them?), and clothes, leaving her with a big fat phone bill.

DOGS AS FRIEND BAROMETERS

A few weeks back my husband and I went to dinner with five other couples. Not all of the couples knew one another so once we finished introductions, our friend Dave said, "OK, you all know Babette and Gordon. Is it safe to assume everyone here has a dog?" The vote was unanimous. Another friend then asked Gordon, "Do you have any friends who don't have a dog?" My husband and I looked at each other and thought about it for a moment. Between us, only one childhood friend doesn't have a dog. Once her children are older, she plans on getting one. The moral of the story is clear: Dog people are the coolest people to have as friends.

Different Paws for Different Women

Just as there are different mates for different women, there are all kinds of dogs for all kinds of women.

All-American Breed Dogs

He may look the same to you. And he may be just as fine, but the next-door dog is the next-door dog and mine—is—mine.

—Dixie Wilson

Some people call these dogs mixed breeds or mutts. I prefer calling them all-American. I am all-American, a mutt of different ethnic backgrounds.

The all-American breed dog comes in a variety of shapes and sizes. All colors and coat types are available. They are relatively inexpensive at your local shelter and usually live very long and healthy lives. Learning and exploring their personalities with them will be a great adventure, much like dating a new partner. Many shelters perform temperament tests on their adoption dogs. Go to a responsible shelter and you will get a lovely companion.

Purebred Dogs

People love purebreds. They know exactly what size and shape the dog will become, as well as have a good idea of the dog's temperament. Purebreds can be more expensive, yet they don't have to be. You can find a purebred dog through a shelter or breed rescue organization. The downside is that you don't always know the parents, but a responsible rescue organization will only adopt dogs with good temperaments. The great part of adoption is that you are saving a life without spending a lot of money. If you don't plan on showing your dog in conformation—the beauty competition in the dog world—adopt one. If you want a puppy, don't dismiss going through rescue. You would be surprised at how many puppies end up in shelters and rescue organizations.

The most popular breeds are not the best for all women. Living situations and lifestyles are some of the factors to consider when choosing a dog. You can find more information on each breed from the parent club for the breed that interests you. The parent club can be found through the American Kennel Club (AKC) at akc.org. The

TRUE STORY

I remember a friend asked for some advice for a friend of hers. Her friend wanted a Labrador Retriever. The guy at the pet store had strongly suggested a Labrador over a Golden Retriever. He just happened to have one in stock. She had a two-and-a-half-year-old at the time as well as a couple of older children. Her concerns were shedding and being good with the children. Labradors are good with children, but young pups can knock very young children down and injure them.

The friend ignored my advice—after all it was free—and instead listened to the man with the vested interest in selling her a puppy. Last week my friend told me how unhappy her friend is with the dog because he sheds everywhere and keeps knocking down her children. She has relegated the dog to the yard. Poor dog. Don't be an airhead. Listen to a vet or an all-breed trainer, not the person who has a vested interest in selling you a dog.

parent clubs, rescue groups devoted to their breed, and responsible breeders are great sources for information on health problems and provide the answers to the questions you need to ask before purchasing that cute pup (see the section "Questions to Ask a Breeder or Anyone Else Who Is Selling You a Puppy" further on). Another excellent source for accurate information on a breed's temperament is a local dog trainer or veterinarian. Ask about specific training and health problems. Be cautious of those that are "breed blind" or have a vested interest in selling you a certain breed. They may sugarcoat any negative traits of a certain breed.

She's Got Personality. Yeah, but What Kind?

Different breeds have different personalities based on the purpose for which they were bred. Most women shop around and investigate a potential mate's, friend's, or boss's personality before committing, but they don't do the same in choosing a dog. If you know what a dog's intended purpose is, you will be more successful in choosing a breed that's right for you. The AKC breaks breeds down by seven groups: sporting dogs, hounds, working dogs, terriers, toys, nonsporting dogs, and herding dogs. In theory, the breeds within each group are similar in function such as hunting or herding, which will dictate similar personalities. However, there are exceptions to these cases and great differences within each group. See Chapter 2 for more information on some of the dogs within each group.

Sporting Dogs
Sporting dogs tend to be the most popular with families and children. They are active dogs that are gregarious and sweet by nature. Happy working or playing with children, they are a great group of dogs.

Hounds
The Hound group is not a group I heartily recommend for women. Although they are easy to groom dogs, they can be exceptionally dif-

ATTENTION GIRLS! POP QUIZ TIME!

Which dog is most likely to help dig up your plants: (1) Golden Retriever, (2) Akita, or (3) Jack Russell Terrier? If you answered 3, that is correct! You may return to your manicure now.

ficult to house-train. Women carry full plates—they take care of children, the dog, the house, their mates, and somewhere they fit in their careers. Why add more work? Keep it simple. However, if you find the right hound dog and start training early, you will do fine.

Working Dogs

Working dogs can be great watchdogs. Most have low grooming needs and generally make calm companions. They have been bred primarily to guard livestock from predators, both human and animal. You can imagine the tenacious characters of these dogs.

Terriers

Terriers are hardy little dogs with lots of chutzpah. Bred as ratters, they often need professional grooming and have lots of energy. Many years ago while training in New York City, I realized there are many terriers in Manhattan. I think people get terriers because of their size and their true Noo Yawk attitude: "Hey, ya gotta problem wit dat, let's take it outside." Like their human counterparts, terriers don't have time to mess around. They have hydrants to spray and other dogs at which to bark, but, dear, they do have to get to their hair appointment—and only at the best spa in town. They are good barkers and agile, active pets. You will dig them!

Toys

Toy dogs are wonderful for women who just want to love something. They make wonderful lap warmers and companions. Children are not necessarily suitable for these dogs because children can play rough and accidentally injure a little dog. Toys can be fulfilling because they just want to be loved and cuddled; they often make great watchdogs as well. The toughest challenge is the difficulty in house-training them.

Non-Sporting Dogs

The non-sporting dogs are a group of dogs that have a little of everything. There are no generalizations when it comes to them, except that none are the same.

Herding Dogs

Herding dogs are my personal favorite group. Overall, they make great watchdogs, have high activity levels, and enjoy lots of training. If you are a mild, quiet person, a herding dog is probably not for you.

Sex and Age

No, this is not an application for the "Dating Game," but you do need to consider whether you want a male or a female dog. Males are more likely to be bossy whereas females will be bitchy, hence the name. There is a higher incidence of aggression in males than in females, and if you already have a male, I would recommend a female. However, males do tend to bond more with the lady of the house.

People always want young puppies, but if you look hard enough you will find a very nice older puppy for your home. Sometimes breeders will get a dog back or decide not to show a dog. You can get a really good dog for a fair price if you keep looking and are open to an older puppy. The advantages are that there will be less puppy mess to clean up because the puppy's probably been house-trained, and you will also spend less money on training and for veterinary care because the puppy has probably been taught some basic skills and has already received her puppy vaccinations.

Don't believe the fallacy that you can't teach an old dog new tricks. Older dogs can be trained to become lovely companions. The next dog I adopt will be a senior citizen. Senior dogs are the most difficult to place in a new home, and although you will have only a few years with the dog, you will be able to give her a happy ending to her possibly not so happy life. It also gives you the opportunity to open your home to more dogs over the years. Strongly consider an older adult or a senior citizen—especially if it is your first dog. You will have an easier time adjusting to the responsibility of a new

SO MANY DOGS. SO LITTLE TIME.

How is a girl to decide? I know, I know. Choosing from all those different breeds isn't easy. Before you decide on a dog or a particular breed, offer to foster a dog for a local rescue organization for a short period of time. This accomplishes several things: you will see how much work a dog really can be, you have fun helping a local rescue organization save a life, and you can also "test-drive" a certain breed of dog you may already have in mind. It is sort of like dating because you don't have to commit. Actually it is better than dating—you don't have to worry about the dog wanting sex from you.

dog, and she will always be grateful to you. When it is her turn to pass over the Rainbow Bridge, she will be shining down on you thanking you for her wonderful last years that you made possible.

Which Dog Will Fit My Lifestyle?

Depending on what type of lifestyle you live and who you are, you may be considering a certain type of dog. There are so many types of women for different dogs and vice versa. But no matter how busy your life or how crowded your home, rest assured that there's a dog out there for you. In my experiences in helping women meet their perfect match, I've noticed different categories of women: single women looking for protection, young married women looking for a family dog, women with young children and older children, empty nesters, divorced women, and widows. Whatever category you fall into, it's important that you have some preliminary information about different breeds, their needs, and their temperaments. In this chapter and the following chapter, you will find an in-depth look at the different breeds I have found suitable for certain needs. (Some of the dogs here may be mentioned as not being good with young children; however, oftentimes it is not that the particular breed isn't good for children but that children are not good for that particular breed. I have also attempted to not recommend high-groom dogs in the categories of women with young children. As a mother, dog grooming will add expense and time to your life, which can become draining.)

Remember that these categories are not set in stone. The important thing is that you do your homework so that you are prepared and choose the perfect dog for you. Once you have settled on one or two breeds, take them each for a test-drive. Offer your local rescue organization to foster that breed for the short term. This will accomplish two things: you can decide if that is the breed for you, and you can also determine whether you really want the responsibility of a dog. It's like dating; you don't have to commit.

Single Women

I'm a lean dog, a keen dog, a wild dog, and lone.

—Irene Rutherford McLeod

The dogs in the list that follow would all make a wonderful companion for a single woman; however, some of them may not be good with children. Even if you don't have children, it is important that you consider whether or not you want a dog that is good with children. There are many factors that can affect a dog's behavior around different children. Some breeds are great around certain children based on a child's age, sex, individual energy level, and personality while other breeds are not as good. For example, a Boxer can be great fun for a big, strong, and active six-year-old boy but overwhelming for a demure little girl, who would probably be much happier with a Bichon Frise. It is imperative that once you find one or two breeds you like that you see how an adult dog of its breed is with children and vice versa.

In the following lists I have inserted an asterisk next to those dogs for which special precautions and extra research are necessary when children will be interacting with these particular breeds. Be certain to read the additional information on these breeds in the next chapter. See also the sections that follow, which identify dogs that are particularly good for children under or over the age of seven.

Affenpinscher*
Afghan Hound
Alaskan Malamute*
American Foxhound
American Staffordshire Terrier
American Water Spaniel
Anatolian Shepherd*
Australian Cattle Dog
Australian Shepherd
Barbet
Basenji*
Basset Hound

Beagle
Bearded Collie
Bichon Frise
Black and Tan Coonhound
Bloodhound
Bolognese
Border Terrier
Borzoi
Boston Terrier*
Boykin Spaniel
Boxer*
Briard

Brittany
Brussels Griffon*
Bull Terrier*
Bullmastiff*
Cairn Terrier
Canaan Dog*
Cavalier King Charles Spaniel
Chesapeake Bay Retriever
Chihuahua*
Chinese Crested*
Clumber Spaniel
Coton de Tulear*
Curly-Coated Retriever
Dachshund*
Dalmatian*
Dandie Dinmont Terrier
Doberman Pinscher*
English Foxhound
English Toy Spaniel*
Finnish Spitz
Flat-Coated Retriever
German Pinscher
Giant Schnauzer
Glen of Imaal Terrier
Great Dane
Greater Swiss Mountain Dog
Harrier
Havanese*
Irish Water Spaniel
Italian Greyhound*
Japanese Chin
Keeshond
Kerry Blue Terrier
Lakeland Terrier
Leonberger
Lhasa Apso*
Löwchen
Maltese*

Mastiff*
Miniature Bull Terrier
Miniature Schnauzer
Newfoundland
Norfolk Terrier
Norwegian Elkhound
Norwich Terrier
Nova Scotia Duck Tolling
    Retriever
Papillon*
Parson Russell Terrier
Pekingese*
Petit Basset Griffon Vendeen
Polish Lowland Sheepdog
Pomeranian*
Poodle (Standard, Miniature,
    and Toy*)
Rottweiler*
Saint Bernard*
Saluki
Samoyed
Schipperke*
Scottish Deerhound
Scottish Terrier
Sealyham Terrier
Silky Terrier*
Skye Terrier
Soft-Coated Wheaten
    Terrier
Spinone Italiano
Staffordshire Bull Terrier
Sussex Spaniel
Tibetan Spaniel
Tibetan Terrier
Welsh Springer Spaniel
Whippet*
Xoloitzcuintli*
Yorkshire Terrier*

A Dog for Protection

You must ask yourself if you want a dog that looks like a protector when you go jogging at night or only to bark and alarm you of anyone outside your home. Certain dogs have a great warning bark but will do nothing if an intruder comes into your home. If a thief saw what was actually barking from behind the door he would laugh. However, police will tell you that any barking dog is enough to tell the crook to break into a different house. The two lists that follow are broken down by dogs that are good barkers and dogs that are very protective or just may look scary (often a large dog's size alone is enough to create a protective appearance). Be cautious of the good barkers. You could get a dog that does not stop barking without training. You will want to train your dog to bark on command and stop when you want her to stop.

GOOD BARKERS

Affenpinscher*
Airedale Terrier
American Eskimo Dog*
American Hairless Terrier
Australian Shepherd
Australian Terrier
Beagle
Bedlington Terrier
Bichon Frise
Bolognese
Border Terrier
Boston Terrier*
Brussels Griffon*
Cairn Terrier
Canaan Dog*
Cavalier King Charles Spaniel
Chinese Crested*
Coton de Tulear*
Dachshund*
Finnish Spitz
French Bulldog
German Pinscher
Havanese*
Irish Terrier
Irish Water Spaniel
Irish Wolfhound
Italian Greyhound*
Lakeland Terrier
Lhasa Apso*
Maltese*
Manchester Terrier (Standard
    and Toy)
Miniature Pinscher
Miniature Schnauzer
Papillon*
Parson Russell Terrier
Pomeranian*
Poodle (Standard, Miniature,
    and Toy*)
Saluki
Schipperke*
Scottish Terrier
Sealyham Terrier

Tibetan Terrier
West Highland White Terrier
Xoloitzcuintli*
Yorkshire Terrier*

PROTECTIVE DOGS
Airedale Terrier
Akbash
Akita
Alaskan Malamute*
American Staffordshire Terrier
American Water Spaniel
Anatolian Shepherd*
Australian Cattle Dog
Belgian Malinois
Belgian Sheepdog
Belgian Tervuren
Bernese Mountain Dog
Bloodhound
Bouvier des Flandres
Boxer*
Briard
Bull Terrier*
Bulldog

Bullmastiff*
Chesapeake Bay Retriever
Dalmatian*
Doberman Pinscher*
German Shepherd Dog
Giant Schnauzer
Golden Retriever
Great Dane
Great Pyrenees*
Greater Swiss Mountain Dog
Irish Wolfhound
Leonberger
Mastiff*
Miniature Bull Terrier
Newfoundland
Norwegian Elkhound
Nova Scotia Duck Tolling
    Retriever
Portuguese Water Dog
Rhodesian Ridgeback
Rottweiler*
Saint Bernard*
Samoyed
Standard Schnauzer

Women with Young Children Under Seven

It is important to remember that young children are not suited for toy dogs. Children can stress a small dog and can also accidentally hurt them. It is a combination I strongly recommend staying away from. The following list includes dogs that can tolerate rambunctious children. However, it is imperative to teach children to play gently with and around all dogs.

American Water Spaniel
Australian Cattle Dog
Barbet
Basset Hound
Beagle

Border Terrier
Boykin Spaniel
Bulldog
Bullmastiff*
Cardigan Welsh Corgi

Cavalier King Charles Spaniel
Clumber Spaniel
English Setter
Field Spaniel
Glen of Imaal Terrier
Gordon Setter
Greater Swiss Mountain Dog
Greyhound
Irish Setter
Irish Water Spaniel
Irish Wolfhound
Keeshond
Lakeland Terrier
Leonberger

Löwchen
Miniature Bull Terrier
Miniature Schnauzer
Newfoundland
Pembroke Welsh Corgi
Portuguese Water Dog
Rottweiler*
Scottish Deerhound
Spinone Italiano
Staffordshire Bull Terrier
Standard Schnauzer
Sussex Spaniel
Tibetan Terrier
Welsh Springer Spaniel

Women with Children over Seven

This category of dogs is more suited to children who are at least seven years old. See the parenthetical notes next to those dogs that are best suited to older children. While you can expect older children to help out in caring for the dog, always keep in mind that you are the main caregiver—no matter what the children promise.

Airedale Terrier
American Hairless Terrier
American Staffordshire Terrier
American Water Spaniel
Australian Cattle Dog
Australian Shepherd
Barbet
Basenji*
Basset Hound
Beagle
Bearded Collie
Bedlington Terrier
Bernese Mountain Dog
Bichon Frise
Bloodhound
Bolognese

Border Collie
Border Terrier
Borzoi
Boxer (for children twelve
    and older)*
Boykin Spaniel
Briard
Brittany
Bull Terrier*
Bulldog
Bullmastiff*
Cairn Terrier
Canaan Dog*
Cardigan Welsh Corgi
Cavalier King Charles
    Spaniel

Chesapeake Bay Retriever

Clumber Spaniel

Collie

Coton de Tulear*

Curly-Coated Retriever

Doberman Pinscher (for
    children nine and older)*

English Foxhound

English Setter

Field Spaniel

Finnish Spitz

Flat-Coated Retriever

Fox Terrier

French Bulldog

German Pinscher

German Shepherd Dog

German Shorthaired Pointer

Giant Schnauzer

Glen of Imaal Terrier

Gordon Setter

Great Dane

Great Pyrenees*

Greater Swiss Mountain Dog

Greyhound

Harrier

Havanese*

Keeshond

Irish Setter

Irish Terrier

Irish Water Spaniel

Irish Wolfhound

Kerry Blue Terrier

Lakeland Terrier

Leonberger

Löwchen

Maltese*

Mastiff*

Miniature Bull Terrier

Miniature Schnauzer

Newfoundland

Norfolk Terrier

Norwegian Elkhound

Norwich Terrier

Nova Scotia Duck Tolling
    Retriever

Otterhound

Parson Russell Terrier

Pembroke Welsh Corgi

Petit Basset Griffon Vendeen

Pharaoh Hound

Polish Lowland Sheepdog

Poodle (Standard, Miniature,
    and Toy*)

Portuguese Water Dog

Rhodesian Ridgeback (for
    teenagers)

Saluki

Samoyed

Scottish Deerhound

Scottish Terrier

Sealyham Terrier

Shetland Sheepdog

Spinone Italiano

Staffordshire Bull Terrier

Standard Schnauzer

Sussex Spaniel

Tibetan Spaniel

Tibetan Terrier

Vizsla

Weimaraner

Welsh Springer Spaniel

West Highland White Terrier

Whippet (for children nine
    and older)*

Born-Again Bachelor Girl

This lady has come a long way, baby—she's a survivor who can overcome any of life's challenges. Perhaps you don't want high maintenance. You want a very nice, loving companion, often a bed warmer.

Affenpinscher*
Airedale Terrier
American Foxhound
American Hairless Terrier
American Water Spaniel
Australian Cattle Dog
Australian Terrier
Barbet
Basenji*
Beagle
Bearded Collie
Bedlington Terrier
Belgian Sheepdog
Belgian Tervuren
Bernese Mountain Dog
Bichon Frise
Black and Tan Coonhound
Bloodhound
Bolognese
Border Terrier
Borzoi
Boston Terrier*
Bouvier des Flandres
Boykin Spaniel
Briard
Brussels Griffon*
Bull Terrier*
Bulldog
Bullmastiff*
Cairn Terrier
Cardigan Welsh Corgi
Cavalier King Charles Spaniel

Chesapeake Bay Retriever
Chinese Crested*
Clumber Spaniel
Curly-Coated Retriever
Dachshund*
English Foxhound
English Toy Spaniel*
Field Spaniel
Finnish Spitz
Flat-Coated Retriever
French Bulldog
German Pinscher
German Shepherd Dog
Glen of Imaal Terrier
Gordon Setter
Greater Swiss
     Mountain Dog
Greyhound
Harrier
Havanese*
Ibizan Hound
Irish Terrier
Irish Water Spaniel
Irish Wolfhound
Italian Greyhound*
Keeshond
Kerry Blue Terrier
Lakeland Terrier
Leonberger
Lhasa Apso*
Löwchen
Maltese*

Manchester Terrier (Standard and Toy)
Miniature Pinscher
Newfoundland
Norfolk Terrier
Otterhound
Papillon*
Pekingese*
Pembroke Welsh Corgi
Pharaoh Hound
Pomeranian*
Poodle (Standard, Miniature, and Toy*)
Schipperke*
Scottish Deerhound

Scottish Terrier
Sealyham Terrier
Shetland Sheepdog
Silky Terrier*
Spinone Italiano
Staffordshire Bull Terrier
Standard Schnauzer
Sussex Spaniel
Tibetan Spaniel
Tibetan Terrier
Welsh Springer Spaniel
Whippet*
Xoloitzcuintli*
Yorkshire Terrier*

Does It Take Two to Tango?

When people think that their older dog doesn't have much time left, they sometimes go out and get a puppy. I have seen this scenario become very difficult for an old friend. Bringing a puppy into a home where there is an old dog can be very stressful for the older dog. Although some older dogs will be revitalized by a new puppy in the house, many won't. If you are serious about getting a puppy, first try getting your older dog around a puppy and see how she reacts. Watch a friend's new puppy for the weekend, or foster a dog for a rescue organization. If you choose not to try it out, wait until your older dog has gone on to a better place before getting the "replacement" dog. I have seen it so many times, and I believe that often it can actually shorten the life of the older dog. Dogs are smart, and your first dog will work out the pack order with the new dog—whether a puppy or an adult. People can be under the assumption that a puppy is an easier adjustment for the older dog that is already in the home. In fact, adding a puppy that needs to be trained and wants to play all day with the old girl can be more stressful for her than an older dog.

And Baby Makes Four

If you are like many people, your dog is your first baby. If you are now pregnant or have just given birth, don't think you should get rid of your dog once you bring your baby home. You simply need to learn how to help your dog adjust to the baby. Your dog has been your devoted best friend; help her enjoy your new blessing by giv-

WELCOMING HOME BABY

The following are tips to help your canine baby prepare for and adjust to your new baby:

1. Buy a crate and get your dog used to it now by feeding her in there. This will create a safe place for her from a baby.

2. Giving your dog flower remedies during the last few weeks of your pregnancy will help soothe her nerves and calm her during the transition. See Chapter 14 for more details on flower remedies.

3. Take five to ten minutes a day for some quality time with your dog—whether it is throwing a ball or teaching her tricks. Once the baby arrives, make sure you give your dog that quality time each day, without the baby. It will be good for you as well as your dog.

4. If your dog has been allowed to sleep on furniture or the bed, this is the time to break that bad habit. Don't wait until the baby arrives.

5. Make preparations for someone to care for your dog when you need to go to the hospi-

tal. You never know how long you will be there, and you want to make sure that someone will be able to get into your home to feed and walk her.

6. Get a crying doll. Practice carrying it around and laying it on the floor to change diapers while you place your dog in a down-stay. Your dog knows the difference between a baby and a doll, but the doll will get her used to something different while she practices staying in one place when you are changing a diaper. Also, your dog will become accustomed to the sound of a baby crying.

7. Start buying baby items right away. You won't drain your pocketbook, and your dog can get used to the new smells and sounds.

8. Most importantly, never ever leave your baby alone with your dog—not even for a second! Take the time to bring the baby or the dog with you into the next room, even if you are just running to get a bottle. Never ever leave them alone together!

ing her the proper guidance. This is best accomplished by consulting with a professional trainer who has personal experience in this area. If you have an aggression problem with your dog, I encourage professional help immediately.

Where Should I Get My Dog?

Shopping is supposed to be fun! But you are not having any fun! You cannot figure out where to get a dog or what to look for when you do find one. Everyone is telling you something different. Shopping the day after Christmas in an outlet mall has to be easier than this! Well, I never said that it would be easy. It will, however, be worth it. There are many places to get a dog, but before you start your search, make a list of the things that are most important to you, for example:

1. saving a life
2. purebred or all-American breed
3. not expensive versus no price too high
4. guarantees
5. health certification and genetic testing of parents

Once you have your list, prioritize the items to help you determine where to get a dog.

The Classifieds

Most people look in their local classified advertisements. This can be Russian roulette in which you might find yourself dealing with the type of breeder who is known as a "backyard breeder." Often these "breeders" purchased a dog and decided to breed their dog to the dog next door, which happens to be the same breed. They might not test for genetic diseases, probably don't understand the breeding for the purpose of improving a breed, want to make their money back on their original purchase, or would just like a puppy from their dog.

REMEMBER THIS STORY

About nine years ago, a family with a German Shepherd puppy hired me. The puppy had a problem with his rear end, and it was obvious from the way it moved that the puppy was dysplastic. I remember talking to the breeder who boasted that she used to show her dogs and that there was nothing wrong with the puppy. I asked her why she no longer showed, and she replied, "Too political." If you ask the people who have been around the dog show game long enough they will tell you the truth. Those that come to a couple of shows and don't win anything will tell you that it is political. Fanciers that have been around showing for years will tell you on any given day that the best dog won. These are the same people who may or may not have a ribbon in their hand that day.

If you decide to go through the classifieds, you may find a dog that is "free to a good home." Use caution here. You may pick up a darling of a dog, but don't believe the reason the owner gives you for needing to find a home. For example, the "needs a yard" excuse is often given because the dog was never properly trained to live in the home. You can certainly train her, but beware that the owner may not be completely honest. The owner may be giving the dog away because she still hasn't been house-trained. By all means, if you have fallen in love with the dog and want her, take her home, but know that you will have to start house-training immediately.

Pet Stores

You can also purchase a dog at a pet store. The media would have you believe that all pet stores sell dogs raised in deplorable conditions when fortunately that is not necessarily the norm. There are high-volume breeding kennels that are immaculate. However, the same drawbacks to buying a dog from the classifieds apply to purchasing a puppy at a pet store with the additional disadvantage that you never get to see the parents nor know their temperament or genetic background. Puppy mills ship puppies all over the country, often through middlemen, who sell to pet shops. You have no idea in which kind of environment the puppy was bred. The important

SMART COOKIE

When you go looking at a litter of puppies, I strongly suggest that you do not bring your checkbook, cash of any amount, or an ATM card. Many puppies have been purchased impulsively by women who just wanted to look. You don't even want the puppy seller to say, "Well, there is an ATM machine down the street." Once you are done looking, go home and sleep on it. If you are meant to have a certain puppy, she will still be there when you go back; otherwise, it wasn't meant to be.

socialization period between seven and sixteen weeks is usually not addressed. Many pet shops will claim to purchase only from "breeders," which is true because whoever owns the dam (the mother) is the breeder.

Don't be fooled by anyone who touts having papers. Papers simply mean that the dog has been registered with a registry body. There are purebred dog registries as well as all-American dog registries.

Breeders

If you are going to get a purebred puppy, contact the AKC at akc.org. The AKC will put you in touch with the parent club of the specific breed you want. The parent club will educate you on the breed and potential health concerns and give you names of breeders. Be sure to ask the parent club which genetic tests the breeder should be doing on the sire and dam (the male and female parents, respectively), such as checking for hip dysplasia or eye cataracts or blood testing for von Willebrand's disease as well as others.

Responsible breeders want to meet you and make sure that getting a dog is the right decision for everyone involved. They will do all types of genetic testing. They breed to improve the breed, not just to make money. They will be involved either in conformation, obedience, agility, or other types of competitive dog activities. They are active in educating themselves about their breed by attending specialties and breed education seminars. Responsible breeders will also take a dog back if you can no longer keep her, which is a huge advantage. They will be available to answer your questions, now and for the life of the dog. Responsible breeders will tend to charge the most for their puppies because they have a lot of money invested in genetic testing and quality breeding. They also offer you their experience within the breed. One word of caution: some breeders appear to be "responsible" but are no better than anyone else. Shop around, do your homework, and thoroughly investigate your options.

QUESTIONS TO ASK A BREEDER OR ANYONE ELSE WHO IS SELLING YOU A PUPPY

1. What kind of personality does the breed have?
2. What is the best kind of environment for this dog? You want to know if this dog will fit into your lifestyle.
3. How does this breed react to children?
4. What are the grooming needs of this breed? Does the dog need a professional groomer? Don't fool yourself into believing that you can do it yourself.
5. What are common health problems? If the breeder tells you that his or her dogs don't have any problems, proceed cautiously. The breeder may not have been breeding long enough.
6. Which genetic tests do you run on your breeding stock? You want the answer to be whatever the parent club recommends.
7. Can I see the certification that you have tested for these conditions/ diseases? If the breeder will only tell you that the vet said everything is fine, I would find another breeder.
8. Can I see both parents? This is rare. Usually you can see the mother but not both because the father usually lives elsewhere. If the breeder tells you that the father or mother is a little "grouchy" or "stressed" due to puppies or people coming in and out, I would be cautious. That may be a sign that the parent's temperament is not very good.
9. Do you show your dogs? In which event? Types of competitions could be anything from agility, obedience, conformation, to field trials. It is very difficult and expensive for any breeder to have his or her breeding stock involved in all types of events, but competition in at least one of the AKC or UKC (United Kennel Club) recognized sporting events demonstrates that the breeder has some type of proving ground for his or her breeding stock. If you can find a breeder whose dogs compete in both conformation and agility/obedience/field trials/herding, you have it made. You have found a breeder who is involved in breeding for both beauty (conformation) and brains (agility/obedience/herding/field trials). This breeder believes in the total dog. A breeder who tells you that showing dogs is political is one who has probably never been able to prove the worth of his or her breeding stock.

WHAT ON EARTH WAS SHE THINKING?

Last year Donna called me wanting help to find a Golden Retriever. She couldn't make up her mind where to get one. I recommended two resources for adoption and several excellent breeders, but she still couldn't reach a decision. Finally, Donna decided she didn't want to spend $800 on a Golden from a breeder who did all of the recommended health clearances. She would rather spend $300 on a dog she found in the newspaper from a breeder who didn't do the routine health clearances. For instance, the parent's hips were not certified, but she didn't mind because she was saving $500. So Donna took Gigi home only to find that Gigi had a thyroid condition as well as several other problems. Within that first year Donna probably spent more than $1,000 in medical expenses on her $300 dog. Had she bitten the bullet and purchased the dog from a reputable breeder she most likely wouldn't have had all the medical expenses. Learn from Donna—before you go out and buy a cheaper dog, find out just how much cheaper the dog really is. If you don't have a lot of money to spend on a dog, go to the local adoption center or breed rescue group. You'll save money, and you'll save a life.

10. Will you take the dog back if for some reason I can no longer keep her? You will hopefully never need to return your dog, but you need to have that security. A breeder who will take a dog back is one who is responsible about his or her breeding practices and puppies.

Adoption Agencies and Rescue Organizations

Another place to get a dog is through an adoption agency, of which, there are several types. Some are breed rescue organizations that are a part of a purebred club. They rescue dogs of that particular breed and put them up for adoption. Often you need to contact the parent club of the particular breed you are looking for, and the club contact person will put you in touch with the local rescue contact. Usually, it is simply a network of breed lovers who foster and rescue dogs awaiting adoption. Other types of adoption agencies may be labeled as adoption centers, humane societies, and shelters.

You can adopt both all-American and purebred dogs through shelters and rescue organizations. Don't believe the old legend that only sick, abused, and aggressive dogs come from shelters. Many shelter dogs are a lot healthier than other dogs. They have built up strong immune systems from being subjected to all sorts of germs because they are housed with many, many dogs. If they are all-American dogs, they have hybrid vigor too. Adopted dogs are often already spayed or neutered and up-to-date on all vaccines and heartworm treatments as well.

If you are concerned about adopting a dog with behavioral issues, don't worry about it. Any dog you get—young or old, purebred or all-American —can have behavioral problems, most of which can be overcome with proper handling and training (see Chapter 14 for more details). In fact, many of these dogs will already be trained to eliminate outside. By adopting you are not only saving a life but you are saving yourself a lot of money and receiving a devoted and thankful companion for many, many good years. So be sure not to overlook these diamonds in the rough.

As is the case with breeders there are responsible and irresponsible dog shelters, so do use caution. Some shelters will attempt to save every dog, which is a very noble cause. However, some dogs are mean and are not able to be rehabilitated. Some shelters, although responsible, may not thoroughly test dogs for stable temperaments before making them available for adoption. Adopting a dog that has aggressive tendencies is a huge liability for you because you just won't know whether the dog will be safe around children and other animals. Just as you would shop around for good car dealers, you should shop around for shelters. You want a shelter that uses temperament testing.

Although there are no guarantees with whichever route you choose, remember a dog is a lifetime commitment, so be sure to take your time and to investigate your options thoroughly. When you finally bring home your new dog, you will know she was worth the wait.

SHELTERS AND TEMPERAMENT TESTING

Sue Sternberg is a trainer from New York. She began working as an animal control officer many years ago and then moved on and began her own shelter and outreach program at her Rondout Valley Kennel in Accord, New York. She is the pioneer in the shelter dog-training movement. One of her vast contributions has been the temperament testing of shelter dogs. It is a solid objective test that stresses the suitability of the dog to live in a home environment. If there is a local shelter that runs this test on all of its dogs, then I would strongly recommend going to that shelter to adopt your new best friend.

The Best Breeds for Women

Opportunities are usually disguised by hard work, so most people don't recognize them.

—Ann Landers

Like lovers, there are so many dogs and so little time. How is a girl to decide? In this chapter I list dogs from each of the seven AKC-recognized groups that will make you a good companion. Remember each breed was bred with an intended work purpose and knowing that purpose will help you determine what the breed's temperament is like. There are many dogs that I didn't list here because I don't think they are necessarily the best for the majority of women. Don't forget you have responsibilities—a career, a social life, maybe children, maybe a partner. You want a dog that can easily be incorporated into your life. The easier the dog is for you, the happier you will be and you will both live in harmony for many, many years. You may decide on a dog that is not discussed here and kudos to you. I would rather be overly cautious than encourage you to get a dog that may not be good for you. If you find that you have chosen a dog that may not be right for you after all, please don't give up on your dog. Seek professional help and allow her to grow out of her puppy habits before you deem the situation hopeless.

For the Sport of It

Generally the sporting dogs are the best dogs to have to meet people. Bred to work next to women, a sporting dog will most likely introduce you to shy people. Sporting dogs tend to think that every human is out there to play with them. You won't have to make the first move; just let your dog make the moves for you. A great thing about sporting dogs and little girls is that these dogs are generally big and love to be hugged. They will tolerate a little girl dressing them up with a hat and sunglasses, which girls love to do. It is more fun to play dress up with their best friend than a doll.

The **Brittany** is a nice dog of medium size. Brittanys are good for children, but they are also extremely active. I wouldn't recommend getting a pet from strong hunting lines. House-training may take patience.

Clumber Spaniels are wonderfully sweet and docile dogs. Though they tend to be slow-moving dogs, they like to have fun. Throw a tennis ball or give the Clumber a child to play with and you will see a tail wagging and a good time being had by all.

The Clumber Spaniel is a preppy type of dog, desired by people who don't want to have the same dog as everyone else. Dog lovers will always come over and ask you what kind of dog you have. Laid-back people tend to be most attracted to Clumbers due to their easy-going looks and personality.

The **German Shorthaired Pointer** is an exceptionally active breed. You must have a lot of patience, for they will literally run circles around you. These sweet dogs are happiest when hunting. Don't try walking one down the street in New York City. She will point to every pigeon she sees. You will never get anywhere.

If you are searching for an outdoorsy partner, be it a friend or a lover, your Brittany or German Shorthaired may help you find one. Both dogs are extremely popular in the hunting world. They are the ultimate dogs for preppies and active outdoor lovers.

The **Golden Retriever** and the **Labrador Retriever** are two entirely different breeds from two different countries. The Golden is from Scotland, and the Labrador is from Canada. I discuss them together to clarify all of the misinformation out there. There is no such thing as a Golden Lab. There are Golden Retrievers and Labrador Retrievers. Labrador Retrievers are known to be Yellow, Chocolate, or Black. The Golden Retriever is a gentleman's gun dog, which was bred in Scotland by Lord Tweedmouth. Originally from New-foundland, the Labrador Retriever is a hardy hunting and retrieving dog capable of withstanding extremely cold temperatures. Many people over the years have told me that they are going to get a Labrador Retriever because a Lab will shed less than a Golden. They are misinformed. They do not shed less! They shed as much, if not more, than a Golden Retriever. The only difference is that the hair is shorter and has a coarser texture. Labradors are good with children; however, in my opinion, Goldens are better than Labradors around smaller children. Labradors are much stronger, much more active, and clumsier than Goldens, and a small child can easily be knocked over by a friendly, well-intentioned Labrador. They are both wonderful breeds. If you have rambunctious boys over the age of seven, the Labrador is fine, but if you have girls or children under seven, go for the Golden. I have owned both over the years and without a doubt, Goldens are easier dogs due to their lower activity level.

If you have your heart set on a Labrador, go to the local Labrador rescue agency and adopt one that is more than two and a half years of age. You can save a life, bypass the insanity of puppy-hood, and enjoy the long life of your devoted new companion. Should you decide to get a Golden, make sure to purchase one from a good breeder who emphasizes temperament. Too many irresponsible breeders have put their priorities in areas other than temperament when breeding, and, unfortunately, you may find that some lines of Golden Retrievers are starting to have aggression problems. Aggression of any form should *not* be tolerated in any breed, especially the Golden Retriever.

You will find that the Lab and the Golden attract all types of people, from computer geeks and construction workers to models, college students, and everyone in between. These gullible love bugs are perfect for hunting, hanging out on the boat, playing at the park, or watching the world pass them by. I remember a beautiful Golden I would see each morning when I lived in New York City. This Golden would carry the bread bag for the owner while she pushed her child's stroller. I think that the Golden ate some pretty awesome bagels each day for breakfast.

The three Setters include the Gordon, the English, and the Irish. The **Gordon Setter** is the most calm with a tendency toward shyness. The **English Setter** is a little bit more active than the Gordon but less so than the Irish Setter. Over the years, I have heard people say that the Irish Setter is stupid. This is a fallacy. The **Irish Setter** is a breed that likes to be kept busy. If you want to find an Irish-Catholic friend, lover, or priest, take an Irish Setter for a walk. Such a person will surely stop to admire the redheaded beauty that is all Irish.

Tall, thin, model-type girls with long flowing hair always look even more beautiful walking next to any of the Setters. If you are built like Gwyneth Paltrow—lucky you!—have thick, long hair, and want a lover, then go with the Setter whose coloring matches yours. If you have just moved to town and want to make some girlfriends, get a different dog. The neighborhood women will find out about you because all of a sudden their husbands are enthusiastically taking out the garbage. You will be talked about at the next moms' club meeting and they will band together and decide whose minivan is going to run over you and your dog.

The most famous **English Springer Spaniel** is Millie, the former first dog of President Bush Sr. and Mrs. Bush. She even wrote a book while serving! A very popular family breed, this dog does require professional grooming, and depending on the breeding of the dog, can have an aggressive streak. Be sure you get the dog from a breeder who is concerned with temperament.

The English Springer Spaniel is a very active dog whose outgoing personality attracts people who like to be on the go and want a small dog that isn't too small.

The **Nova Scotia Duck Tolling Retriever** is a great dog. They are small yet very agile. They are good with children and don't need excessive grooming. Regular brushing will be sufficient for a Toller. True hunters love this dog. Although the Toller is a bit uncommon now, I predict this dog will become the next family dog, especially in large cities and high-density residential communities. The Toller will attract those who dare to be different and want to set trends.

Vizslas are sweet and smart. When you train one, you will see the wheels in her head spinning as she tries to figure out how to do it her way. If you are too easygoing, your Vizsla will train you in no time. They are very clean dogs and do not require a lot of grooming. The Vizsla will attract outdoorsy types, neat and tidy people, and athletes alike.

Weimaraners have been made famous by photographer William Wegman. When the breed first became popular in the United States in the 1950s, the dogs were touted as being "born housetrained." They are great watchdogs, good with children, and easy to train, as long as you start when they are young. Since they do have a high activity level, it is important that you start training them as puppies. The Weimaraners' only drawback is that as they get older they can become a little grouchy with other animals.

This breed attracts active, outgoing people who have a rather "go with the flow" approach to life. Their neat and clean appearance will also attract any type of dog lover who loves dogs but not their hair.

HOW DUMB IS YOUR DOG?

Several breeds in the sporting group have been called dumb—not just by owners but those who should know better as well. I remember an owner said to my dad, "This dog is so stupid." My dad asked, "Is she running your life?" The owner emphatically said, "Yes, she is." My question to you is if she was running that woman's life, how stupid could the dog be? She sounds like a pretty smart dog to me. There are no stupid dogs or breeds. You just have to approach the training differently for different dogs. I am saddened when anyone says any breed or individual dog is stupid. Before you decide that your dog is dumb, think about who is outsmarting who.

Ain't Nothin' but a Hound Dog

A huge asset to the hound dog group is that most hound dogs are wash-and-wear, which saves you time and money on professional grooming. The hound group is not as outgoing as the sporting dogs—

they are much happier hanging around or hunting for prey. So if you want to use a hound dog as mate bait, you will depend on the catch to make the first move. Rest assured your hound dog will melt the heart of anyone who stops to say hello.

Basset Hounds are adorable dogs. People recognize them as Hush Puppies. They can make a great apartment dog, but you must be cautious and start training immediately to stop any howling problems from developing. They are rabbit-hunting dogs from France. They are also used in the United States to track and hunt rabbits. Hunters love the sound of the Basset's howl, which is known to them as "mountain music," because the howling means the dogs are hot on the trail of the game. Yet your next-door neighbor may not enjoy mountain music, which is why it is important to train your Basset not to howl early on. They are very sweet and funny and get along well with other dogs, but they may have a need for some extra doggy perfume, as well as extra tissues for a little bit of drool. You will need to have a lot of patience for house-training too.

People who appreciate big, sad eyes and soft, droopy ears will always want to say hello to your Basset, while those who are turned off by dog odors or drool will not be inclined to say hello.

Beagles are good with children, but a woman will have the same challenges with Beagles as she would with a Basset: house-training and "mountain music." Beagles originated in Great Britain and are more agile and energetic than the Basset.

Any Snoopy fan will want to say hello to your Beagle. If the person is shy, your Beagle will quite possibly make the introductions.

Dachshunds are great little dogs with lots of chutzpah. The downside, like most hounds, is that they can be difficult to house-train if you don't start immediately. They do well with paper-training. They can be great little watchdogs since they love to bark, but again, make sure your neighbor doesn't mind the "urban music" your Dachshund plays.

Even people who are intimidated by dogs will be more likely to say hello to a little dog. Children will rush over to your Dachshund, so use caution for her happiness and security. You don't want a well-intentioned child to scare her causing her to bite.

Greyhounds are a wonderful breed and one I strongly recommend for women. All types of personalities are good for these low-maintenance, clean dogs. They are very gentle, so be cautious if you have rowdy, hard-playing young children. You don't want the children's good fun to frighten your Greyhound. Contrary to popular belief, Greyhounds do make great apartment dogs. They like to just lounge around and look magnificently regal. Yes, they do like to run too, so make sure to run them within a secure fenced-in area to keep them safe. They can startle easily, which can cause them to run off. Retired racing Greyhounds have been trained to run at the sound of a gunshot, so use caution as a car backfiring could trigger their running instinct.

Since Greyhounds are not exceptionally gregarious dogs, don't depend on them to make the introductions to friends and potential lovers. You will need to break the ice. Usually thin-framed people are found with these dogs as well those who tend to be quiet, intelligent, and a bit on the logical side of the brain, such as engineers or accountants.

The **Norwegian Elkhound** is a good watchdog. These dogs like to work; their original purpose was as a guardian and herder but also for hunting elk. This hardiness makes them tolerant with rough children.

Petit Basset Griffon Vendeens are very active dogs that are really a large dog in a smaller package. They do require regular visits to the doggy hair salon and spa.

This dog attracts preppy, outgoing people who like to kick back and have a good time while having a taste for the finer and more unique things in life.

Rhodesian Ridgebacks are beautiful and strong watchdogs. I don't recommend them, however, for many women, due to their tenacity and stubbornness. They will be more apt to listen to a man. The Ridgeback is a low-maintenance dog that is easy to bathe and keep clean. They can be good in a house with teenaged children

VERY IMPORTANT LESSON

Joan is a lovely lady who I worked with several years ago. She had adopted a retired racing Greyhound and took him outside with her one night to put out the trash; her screen door slammed shut behind them and off he went. She found him three weeks later about fifteen miles away on the other side of the interstate and eighteen pounds thinner. How he got to that side of town without getting killed she never knew, but they were glad to have found each other. When she called me to tell me he was missing, I explained how the slamming of the door sounded like a gunshot—the signal at which the dog had been trained to run, so he ran. There are wonderful Greyhound rescue organizations that can help you get a retired racing dog. If you choose one, be sure your dog is always confined to a fenced-in area.

because they are strong and robust. Getting knocked around by your seventeen-year-old son would be a lot of fun for both the dog and your son.

You will find that independent, self-assured people love these elegant dogs. Men who like to walk into a room and make a statement enjoy having a Ridgeback by their side. People who like to "speak softly and carry a big stick" enjoy being around Ridgebacks. If you are looking for a mate, you will definitely find one with this beauty. Rest assured, girlfriend, that with this beautiful breed you will meet an independent, confident partner.

Whippets are nice dogs and make lovely companions, but children younger than nine may be too rough and rambunctious for one. Remember, if you are a single woman, you want a breed that will be good with babies should you decide to have one in the next fifteen years. Whippets are very low-key dogs and perfect for a small apartment. Whippets tend to attract the same type of person who is attracted to a Greyhound.

Dogs Working for a Living

Working dogs can be great watchdogs. Most grooming needs are generally just a daily brushing. Fancy hairstyles and trips to the spa are not the norm for these calm companions. Working breeds can do well with young children, provided they have stable temperaments and are well-trained. Due to their high tolerance for pain, these dogs can tolerate boys running and slamming into them or being accidentally hit with a toy. They will also tolerate—within reason—a gentle girl climbing all over them and hugging and hanging on them endlessly. Nevertheless, always monitor playtime with the dog. This is for both the dog's and the children's protection.

The **Akbash Dog** is not for the fainthearted. These dogs have a reserved but protective nature and should thus be introduced to other animals and children when young. They are great dogs if you live on a cattle farm or horse ranch and need protection for your livestock. You will need to have a very strong personality for this type of dog.

To attract a friend or mate with the Akbash, you will undoubtedly only attract people who truly love and appreciate dogs. The Akbash will most likely intimidate those with soft personalities. Bounty hunters or prosecuting attorneys who have a taste for the unusual will most likely ask you about your dog.

The **Alaskan Malamute** is powerful. Known for their howling talent and digging in the yard for diamonds—woman's other best friend—Alaskan Malamutes can be very tough. I knew one that not only escaped from her fenced-in yard, but then climbed the fence of the yard across the street and attacked and injured two German Shepherds at the same time. This was a female, or a bitch as we call them, which is not the sex most frequently known to be aggressive.

Strong, athletic people tend to admire the Malamute. Those who are intimidated by larger, stoic dogs will keep their distance, until they get to know your dog.

The **Anatolian Shepherd** is one heck of a guard dog. I would only recommend this dog if you are a strong owner and will not allow the dog to run your home.

The **Black Russian Terrier** hasn't yet been recognized by the AKC, but in my opinion is a working dog. These dogs were developed by the Russian military in the 1930s using Rottweilers, Giant Schnauzers, Airedale Terriers, and Newfoundland mixes.

They are tenacious but gentle. Protective of their families, Black Russian Terriers are good with children because they are willing to tolerate a lot of excitement.

Boxers are a pleasure. They can be stubborn, but, for the most part, they enjoy pleasing their owner. Older children, particularly boys twelve and older, are preferred with these low-maintenance guard dogs. Due to their activity and roughness in play, they can be overpowering for a very delicate little girl.

These goofy, loveable, and fun dogs will attract anyone who wants to have fun, doesn't mind drool, and likes a strong personality. Boxers and anyone walking with one make a statement.

Doberman Pinschers are very terrier-like in their attitudes. This stunning breed is very trainable and enjoys working. They can look very menacing and are good watchdogs but most often are sweethearts. Children nine and up are good companions for the Doberman. Since Dobermans don't like to sit still for very long, boys would

DID YOU HEAR ABOUT THE PAPERS?

Some people will get so excited about "papers." Papers mean nothing; well, that is not completely true. A dog with papers means someone paid a registry body to record the breeding of the dog. I can become my own kennel club or registry body. Send me twenty bucks, and I will give you a pretty piece of paper saying I verify what you told me is true. So if you want papers, send me the money and I will send you some. You will be the very first person to be registered in the Chien du Babette Kennel Club— ooh la la! Tell your puppy she is a French-registered dog! You can then teach her how to stick her nose up in the air on cue.

Unless you have plans on showing your dog, don't worry about the papers. They don't guarantee quality; they only state that your dog is a purebred.

enjoy them more than girls. They can also be very protective of their owners. As long as they are given enough activity, Dobermans can do well in an apartment.

Yes, you will intimidate anyone who doesn't know any better with your Doberman, but if you want to attract someone who is a biker, construction worker, or just has a strong, down-to-earth personality, then the Doberman is for you.

Giant Schnauzers are great all-around watchdogs albeit a little stubborn. They do well with all types of people. Since they are not very active or clumsy, you wouldn't have to worry about them knocking down your children.

Some people may be intimidated by the sheer size of Giant Schnauzers, but these dogs aren't as tough-looking as other working breeds. They are, however, stoic and just as tough as the others so do not be deceived. Giant Schnauzers are loved by trendsetters and rough-and-tumble, outdoorsy types alike.

Great Danes are very elegant dogs. Their calm nature and very low grooming needs make them a nice guard dog for a family. However, aggression can be a problem within the breed. Make certain to research the pedigree of the puppy. As with any breed, you want to meet both the parents and other dogs that have come from a previous breeding, if possible.

You will find that people who like to walk around with a Great Dane enjoy clearing a path for them and their dog. Think about how a city sidewalk clears for a Great Dane. People stop and watch this horse of a dog walk down the street. I remember walking one of my students down Worth Avenue in Palm Beach. All of the people carrying shopping bags had to move out of Merlin's way. Merlin was the talk of the street. He garnered so much attention that I heard he was the talk at Trump's Mar-A-Lago club that evening.

Great Pyrenees can shed and drool a bit so they are best with women who don't mind some mess. They do well with children and are easygoing in nature.

Due to the softer appearance and laid-back attitude of these dogs, burly types are not as likely to be attracted to them as they would be to a Mastiff, for example. However, people who love cuddling with something soft, yet want to make a statement or feel protected wherever they go, will gravitate toward the Pyrenees.

Newfoundlands are wonderful dogs. Very sweet and gentle, they are great apartment dogs despite their size. They have a very low activity level, are good watchdogs, and are just terrific with children. They make great family companions. Pick up a historical book on the Newfie and you will find many accounts of this wonderful breed saving people. Sir Edwin Landseer was an artist who painted a Newfie having saved a little girl from drowning. This painting is aptly named "Saved." Sir Edwin Landseer enjoyed painting the black and white Newfoundland so much that there is now a color known as "Landseer."

These dogs attract people who just want a soft dog to cuddle and sleep with next to the fire, people who love the great outdoors and want a hiking companion, or people who want a dog that gives an intimidating impression. Due to their size, they can create quite an illusion, especially with people who may be afraid of dogs. Yet, people who admire sweet dogs will be more than happy to meet your gentle Newfoundland.

Portuguese Water Dogs are another breed I recommend to those who want a low-shed dog. These dogs do hold their coat, however, and the dead hair needs to be brushed out regularly. It is a terrific breed for a young woman or empty nester and great for children. They are very active, sweet, and very trainable. They also make good watchdogs.

Let's set the record straight on **Rottweilers**. Rotties, as they are affectionately called, are great dogs, but they are *not* for most people. Unfortunately, much indiscriminate breeding has really affected the true temperament of this wonderful breed. Rotties have become victims of negative press due to a few dogs with very ignorant and irresponsible owners. Males can be stubborn and tough.

Although they would be good around children, children are not necessarily going to be good around them. Go to a responsible breeder and meet the parents. You will pay more for your puppy but at least it won't be for a lawsuit or hospital bill.

Rottweilers are awesome dogs—tough on the outside, but laid-back on the inside. Unfortunately, if you are walking down the street with a Rottweiler, chances are you won't have too many people running up to meet you. The media has portrayed them to be something they aren't. When you hear of a Rottweiler attacking a child, it is a terrible tragedy, but you have to look at the statistics. There are more Rottweilers than any other breed in the United States; therefore, you are going to have more chances for a dog bite. Rottweilers are tenacious, but they can also be very gentle and affectionate creatures.

I own a Rottweiler. Lili came to live with us after her owner, who hired us to train her, had to leave and go back to Europe. When it comes to my rambunctious two-year-old son, she is very gentle. Lili is capable of creating trouble for some ill-intentioned fool when it comes to her family, but she also knows that although she doesn't rule the house, she certainly protects it. It is very important that your Rottie be given a set of rules to live by. If your Rottie doesn't respect you or the rules or has temperament problems, you are in trouble. Get good professional help immediately.

If you want to scare away your neighbors, get a Rottie. Your Rottie may also scare off potential lovers and friends unless you prefer the rougher, tougher types.

Saint Bernards have been one of many breeds that have received the Hollywood curse. The movie *Beethoven* has led many to believe that Saint Bernards are fun, sweet, intelligent dogs that are easy to train and great with kids. Unfortunately, this is not entirely true. They are intelligent, but they can be very stubborn. As they get older they can become a little on the aggressive side. It is one thing to have a Chihuahua bite you, but it is much worse when a Saint Bernard bites. Due to the breed's potential for surliness or stubbornness, you would do better with a female than a male. Make sure you don't mind the tremendous amount of drooling that comes with the Saint Bernard and understand that they get huge: they can weigh as "little" as 140 pounds and as much as 180 pounds. I was at the local shelter one day not too long ago. There was a young Saint Bernard in the kennel. Her identification card read that the owners had turned her in because she "got too big." If you want a giant breed of dog, make certain you truly understand the size the puppy will become so that your dog doesn't end up like this one. Meet several full-grown ones and even watch a friend's for the weekend to be sure you can handle a huge dog.

Anyone who has children will recognize Beethoven when you walk her down the street. Kids will come running and people who don't mind drool will love to meet you and your laid-back Beethoven.

Samoyeds are very active, high-groom dogs. It is best to be able to stay one step ahead of this very bright breed. Due to their size and activity level, Samoyeds are best around boys. They may overwhelm little girls and knock them down.

The thick white fur of a Samoyed attracts many dog lovers, particularly athletic, outdoorsy people. Yet Samoyeds cannot be depended upon to introduce you to new people, as they enjoy performing tasks more than playing social director.

The **Standard Schnauzer** is a beautiful dog of medium size. These dogs can be active and feisty. You will need to remind your Schnauzer that you make the rules and she must abide by them.

These dogs can attract people who want nothing but the best and enjoy a bit of status. People with lots of spunk also appreciate these dogs. Standard Schnauzers are oftentimes more interested in chasing other dogs then they are in greeting people.

Terriers: Big and Small, You Will Dig Them All

Terriers are great matchmakers. Very social, terriers will always introduce you to other dogs—and their owners! Terriers can be great companions for young exuberant boys. They are active and like to play roughly but aren't likely to knock anyone down. Little girls can get frustrated with a terrier because they want to love and hug the dog, but terriers are more likely to run around them barking, which will be encouraged by a little girl's high-pitched voice.

The **Airedale Terrier** is the largest of all terriers. This breed was one of the first used for police work in Germany and Great Britain, and they served in the forces during wartime as well. Like most terriers they have a high energy level. They are very rambunctious and good with children. They do well playing ball with boys or just roughhousing and climbing all over each other. Be prepared to take your Airedale to a groomer on a regular basis.

You will find that many people in the sixty-plus age range will automatically bond with your Airedale. It was quite a popular child's dog many years ago. President Kennedy shared the White House with one. Stylish, intelligent, self-assured people are very attracted to this terrier.

Australian Terriers are small dogs that do well in small apartments. Quite scrappy, they were bred as ratters but were at times used to guard mines, tend sheep, and serve as personal watchdogs. Due to their small size, Australian Terriers and children are not always the best combination. Rambunctious boys can run and accidentally step on the dog, harming the dog or tripping themselves. Young girls with their high voices will scream with delight prompting a lot of barking from your little friend. These dogs may also dig holes in your yard.

Movers and shakers love the Australian Terrier's delightful attitude. With her nonthreatening size yet amiable courage your Australian Terrier will help you approach most friends you haven't met yet.

The **Bedlington Terrier** is highly skilled as a hunter of badgers, fox, otters, and rats. They are very sturdy dogs that don't get much bigger than twenty-three pounds.

Even though they won't make the first move with people, Bedlington Terriers will draw curious onlookers with their unusual appearance. Those who are not very interested in dogs may even ask what kind of dog you have.

The **Border Terrier** hails from the northeastern border of England and Scotland. Farmers needed a terrier to hunt fox. The

PIT BULLS ARE WONDERFUL DOGS

Bet you never knew! Pit Bulls are awesome dogs! Huh? Now this is one part of this book I hesitated putting in. Why, you ask? Well there is a lot of misinformation and ridiculous legislation passed by ignorant bureaucrats. It is sort of a catch-22. If they had the correct information, they wouldn't pass such ridiculous breed-specific legislation. After all, they could never pass legislation against certain types of humans, could they? Well, maybe legislation against mean people wouldn't be such a bad idea.

What exactly is a Pit Bull anyway? That alone can become several books, so I want to keep it simple. Pit-type dogs are dogs that have been bred to fight one another in the pits. Dog fighting is a disgusting sport. It is a felony, yet you can still find it in pockets of the United States where gambling and drugs go hand in hand.

Pit fighting dogs are bred to be tenacious and courageous with other dogs; however, aggression with humans is not tolerated. Contrary to popular belief, aggression with other dogs doesn't translate into aggression with humans, in any breed.

Pit Bull-type dogs include the following: American Pit Bull Terrier, American Staffordshire Terrier, Staffordshire Bull Terrier, Bull Terrier, and Miniature Bull Terrier. They are separate breeds with differing personalities, but they have a common history of being bred to fight other dogs. It has been more than sixty years since dog fighting was declared illegal, so it is safe to assume that much of the "fight with other dogs to the death" gene has been diluted. Do not misunderstand, however; they will still be tough, but since they are no longer bred for this illegal and despicable "sport," it is somewhat safe to assume that their drive to fight is not as strong as it once was. Nevertheless, should you choose one of these dogs, get her used to playing with other dogs immediately.

Pit Bull-type dogs are wonderful dogs. They are very sweet with humans, can tolerate a lot of abuse from children, and are very easy to train. Behaviorally they do not tend to have difficult problems. They are healthy and live long happy lives.

small Border Terrier was perfect because of their speed, which not all terriers have, and their ability to take the fox to ground.

Most people will think your Border Terrier is an all-American dog. They are not common and look like a cute little mixed breed. If someone strikes up a conversation with you, he or she will undoubtedly admire the unusual characteristics of your Border Terrier.

Bull Terriers are either white or brindle in color. They are very cool dogs and exceptionally bright. Originally used as pit fighting dogs, they can be very animal aggressive. It is important that they are trained and managed properly.

Bull Terriers are always recognized by the thirty-plus crowd, thanks to Spuds McKenzie. The Budweiser dog attracts sports enthusiasts as well as former college and high school party animals. If you are trying to get the attention of a football fan or former brother of Delta Kappa Epsilon (Toga! Toga!), then the Bull Terrier may be a good dog for you.

Cairn Terriers owe their recognition to Toto and Dorothy. The breed's yellow brick road started on the Isle of Skye in northwest Scotland. This dog was developed in the early 1800s to hunt small game, such as otter and fox.

Every fan of *The Wizard of Oz* will talk to you about your Toto. This is an excellent breed to have if you want to meet people.

Fox Terriers include the **Smooth Fox Terrier** and **Wirehaired Fox Terrier**, which were very popular thirty years ago. Many wealthy people had these two breeds because they were great to take on a hunt.

Think of the typical old-money type of person who lives in Charlottesville, Virginia, where the hunt is still alive and well. Older people love to meet these dogs because they were such popular dogs way back. Young, conservative folks will also gravitate toward Fox Terriers, as will any well-heeled individual.

The **Manchester Terrier** comes in two sizes: the Toy weighs less than twelve pounds, and the Standard weighs between twelve and twenty-two pounds. They both make great watchdogs. If a child is too rough with them, they may try to protect themselves by nipping. These wash-and-wear dogs make a good pet for women who have the tenacity to keep up with their antics and not allow them to control the home.

Your outgoing Manchester Terrier will attract many potential friends and mates. They look like tough little dogs, so even macho men will appreciate them.

The **Miniature Schnauzer** is a very popular breed with empty nesters. They make great apartment companions and terrific watchdogs with their ferocious bark. They can be good with children. They like to learn new things but will come up with various antics when not kept busy. Be prepared to make your dog salon appointment as often as you make your own hair salon appointment, perhaps even more often. Like the Standard and Giant Schnauzers, the Miniature attracts vibrant people who love an unusual looking dog.

Norfolk and **Norwich Terriers** are scrappy little dogs that are perfect for city living. Since they have lots of personality, people adore them. They are great watchdogs but require frequent visits to the spa.

Very friendly and cute-as-a-button, these terriers will make even non-dog lovers laugh at their metropolitan attitude as they strut down the street letting everyone know they have "arrived."

Formerly known as the Jack Russell Terrier, the **Parson Russell Terrier** has been thrust into the limelight thanks to the canine star Eddie of "Frasier." Everyone will expect your spunky dog to be the brightest on the block. Don't be lulled into thinking they will train themselves and will be as well-behaved as Eddie—not without a lot of work. They can be bossy with other dogs, love to run off and ignore you, and will dig out of the yard. They need lots of training and guidance.

Young and old, male and female, everyone you meet will recognize your Parson Russell. These popular dogs with lots of gusto have all types of admirers.

The **Scottish Terrier**, affectionately known as the Scottie, is an active dog with lots of gusto, and they can be great for rambunctious little boys. They are not wash-and-wear so be prepared for frequent visits to the doggy spa. Be confident that should another dog pick on your Scottie, she will be able to hold her own and even teach the big dog a thing or two.

West Highland White Terriers are also tough with other animals but are great with rough boys. Westies may be little, but they are also strong so I recommend them for people with boys older than nine years. While they have the potential to boss around other dogs, they are not as bossy as a Bull Terrier.

IT'S SEX EDUCATION TIME, GIRLS!

Make sure you have your dog neutered as soon as she is six months old. The three correct terms are *spay* for a female, *castrate* for a male, and *neuter* for either sex. If you want to score points with a guy, don't use the word *castrate*. They hate it! They think dogs are as attached to their reproductive organs as they are. Use the word *neuter* instead.

Both Westies and Scotties are the ultimate preppy dogs. They have lots of attitude and have a fun time saying hello to everyone—big and small. You will attract any Brit too, since they are very popular in Great Britain.

Toys Love to Be Babied

If you are going on a man hunt, these dogs won't help that much. These are the dogs that most men will not consider "real dogs," until they get to know them. Once they have given their hearts to a little dog, men aren't too embarrassed to admit it. Women of course are immediately drawn to these small bundles of love. Children and most toys, however, are not the best combination because children can stress small dogs or hurt them by accident through rough play. Toys do well in the city or the country, but they are sometimes difficult to house-train.

The **Affenpinscher** is a scrappy little dog whose claim to fame is Jack Nicholson's archenemy in the Academy Award–winning movie, *As Good as It Gets*. Affenpinschers have lots of personality and are very active just like a terrier. They make great watchdogs but do not do well with children. Children have high-pitched voices, which can be stressful to them. Affenpinschers like things to be quiet. They just want the attention focused on them and for everyone to do as they see fit.

Brussels Griffon is very similar to the Affenpinscher. These dogs evolved from a cross between the Affenpinscher and the Belgian Street Dog. They are good watchdogs but do not thrive around children for the same reasons that Affenpinschers don't.

The people that I see attracted to both the Affenpinscher and the Brussels Griffon are true dog lovers. These dogs always charm them with their unique looks and loveable personalities. If you are rather shy, these two confident and outgoing breeds will help you meet real dog people.

The **Cavalier King Charles Spaniel** is one of my all-time favorite dogs. They have wonderful personalities and make great watchdogs. Their one drawback is that they can be difficult to house-train like most toy dogs. When people tell me they want a dog like a Golden Retriever but smaller, Cavalier King Charles is my first recommendation. They are very sweet and patient dogs, which makes them a good breed for gentle children. They will tolerate your daughter playing wardrobe designer and allow her to tirelessly put outfit after outfit on them. The Cavalier will stay in a carriage while being pushed around town wearing sunglasses. They also will chase the ball throw after throw for your boy and are more than happy to learn tricks easily for any child. Although active they won't get so excited that they will knock down little people like larger active dogs might who do not realize their own strength.

These lovely toy-sized spaniels will introduce you to just about anyone who walks down the street. If they steer clear of a stranger, you can be assured that he or she isn't a dog person. Even macho types can be charmed by the glimmer in these dogs' eyes coupled with their charisma.

The **Chihuahua** is mass marketing's latest victim. The Taco Bell dog is definitely not good with children, but they are excellent watchdogs with lots of personality. However, they can have aggression problems when they aren't bred, trained, and socialized properly. Both the Long Coat and Smooth Coat varieties are easy to maintain and can be bathed easily in the kitchen sink. It will take you longer to wash your own hair, than their whole body.

Kids will recognize your little friend. Many men will not think she is really a dog, but true dog lovers will definitely comment on your Mexican companion. Don't depend on your amiga to introduce you to people; the Chihuahua is a real girl's girl. These dogs believe in playing hard to get.

The **Coton de Tulear** is another gorgeous dog. Don't let their delicate appearance fool you; they are filled with spunk and personality. I know of four that most appropriately live in Palm Beach. The owner is very kind and these high-maintenance dogs with their long, flowing silky coats actually match their spacious contemporary home. Able to hold their own, they rule the bike path and there is no chance anyone will ever be able to break into that home quietly. They look like prima donnas, but they have a lot to say.

English Toy Spaniels can be a rather aloof and calm dog. Due to their temperament they are not the friendliest dogs and are not amused by children, nor do they care to guard your home. They make excellent lapdogs and enjoying lying in your lap while you brush or stroke them.

Gentle, quiet souls tend to be the most attracted to these dogs. Your grandmother would love one as a lap warmer.

Another **Fox Terrier**, the **Toy Fox Terrier**, is rather difficult to house-train. A gregarious breed, they are sweet, happy dogs and enjoy trick training. However, they are not well suited to children, who can pose a danger to their light build and small bones.

Believe it or not, I have been fortunate enough to work with quite a few members of the **Havanese** breed. I know a prominent family who spends the winter in Palm Beach who started a local epidemic of Havanese ownership. I have often thought about adding this intelligent breed to my family; however, it would be unfair to subject a small dog like the Havanese to the rambunctious antics of my toddler. Not a mainstream breed until very recently, this dog is fun-loving, friendly, easy to train, and enjoys daily hair brushing and pampering at the spa on a regular basis. They can make great little watchdogs and are a bit sturdier than most toy dogs. Early training is critical. They can become aggressive as they get older if they were not properly trained while young.

People who have champagne taste love to admire the beauty of these silky little dogs. You will also find Cubans and lovers of Hispanic culture—male and female alike—are greatly attracted to these dogs. Many can be very friendly with strangers, but there are many who are not interested in meeting new people. There is some aggression in this breed. With their attitude these dogs will certainly let you know when someone is approaching you on your walk and will protect you more than you can imagine given their size.

Italian Greyhounds are wonderfully sweet dogs. These demure dogs have a very delicate frame and can be easily hurt not only by a child playing and running around but by an adult as well. I remember a very nice grandmother who had one named Romeo. One day he wiggled out of her arms and fell, breaking his leg. These dogs have a wonderful spirit for quiet, older women who live alone.

One physical characteristic I have noticed about Italian Greyhound lovers is they all seem to be petite, refined women although the number of fans of this breed is certainly not small. These quiet, timid dogs will open up to any person who greets them, but until then, they will keep to their dainty selves because sometimes the world is just nicer to sit and watch.

Japanese Chins are easy-to-groom dogs that require low amounts of exercise. They can be difficult to house-train. Since they don't bark, they don't make effective watchdogs.

Primarily quiet, gentle dogs, they will help you meet lots of nice women, but if you want to meet a guy—forget about it. Men generally don't gravitate toward small dogs unless they have lots of spunk and attitude.

The **Maltese** has lots of personality. These dogs love to be trained, and house-training is a breeze if you start early. They are very friendly, sweet, and energetic little dogs. Barking can develop into a large problem if it is not addressed in puppy-hood. They also need to be brushed daily and taken to the dog spa often. Don't be fooled by the prima donna look of the Maltese. They are tough little dogs that can certainly hold their own. I have even seen them back down German Shepherds.

I think all women ooh and aah over the Maltese because they are so pretty. This is another dog, however, that will not necessarily help you meet a man, but the Maltese has been known to have male admirers.

I remember when Jimmy Buffet's wife called asking for help for her Maltese. My husband, doubting that she was the wife of *the* Jimmy Buffet, said, "Jimmy Buffet would not have a Maltese." I then rattled off several different very good-looking men with sexy wives who not only had a Maltese but also loved them to death. All of these men were financially successful, very cool, hip, down-to-earth, sincere men. After I jogged my husband's memory, he even admitted that if he were to have a little dog, he would have a Maltese or a Bichon. I hope he remembers that when I am ninety years young and want a small dog.

Given the fact that the **Miniature Pinscher** was originally bred as a ratter, it is no surprise that they make excellent watchdogs. Miniature Pinschers and children are not necessarily the perfect combination, so it is important that children are taught what they should learn with every dog: do not bother the dog when she is sleeping and do not tease her. Miniature Pinschers have a very high activity level and make nice low-maintenance companions for anyone who is not willing to allow them to run the roost but is willing to exercise them often. If you live in a small apartment, be prepared for them to redesign it if they are not given early training.

The Miniature Pinscher attracts outgoing people who really love big dogs in small packages. They are social and active so they will make it easy for you to start a conversation with just about anyone. The cute guy next door will be a lot more apt to talk to you about your dog than if you had one of the "sissy" toy breeds.

A single woman once asked me to tell her about the **Papillon**. Would it make a good pet for her? Yes, Papillons are sweet dogs that have a playful attitude and are good with older children who are taught to be gentle with animals. Small children are a no-no for Papillons as an unknowing child can injure them easily. Since they have a propensity to bark, they make great watchdogs, but it is important to train your Papillon so that when you don't want her to bark any longer, she stops.

The **Pekingese** is a Chinese breed that likes a calm, quiet environment, preferably on your lap, and enjoys being brushed daily. If you want a watchdog this is not the dog for you. These dogs are not suited to children since children can injure the dogs' eyes easily.

Since the Pekingese is not a very common breed, many people will be curious as to what kind of dog you have. Don't be insulted, however, if they tell you some mop jokes. That is bound to happen with a Peke.

The **Pomeranian** is a dog with tons of personality. These very happy-go-lucky dogs are fun to watch as they perform their antics; however, due to their diminutive size, these dogs aren't well suited to rambunctious children. Make sure that you are willing to brush them each day. This is another dog that needs to be trained not to bark whenever she wants. Pomeranians sound like squeak toys when they bark, which can really agitate larger dogs, which in turn can start a fight that a Pomeranian is certain to lose.

This is one dog that attracts people. They are vibrant, beguiling dogs that can introduce you and themselves to anyone within fifty yards without giving it a thought. Believe it or not, they do charm big, tough guys as well, probably because their attitudes are big and tough.

I can't say enough good things about **Poodles**, no matter their size, **Toy**, **Miniature**, or **Standard**. This is an awesome breed that has more tenacity than men and some women are willing to believe. The Poodles' only drawback is that they are very high-maintenance dogs needing regular visits to the groomer. They are very easy to train but will bark a lot if allowed. Young children are not recommended for Toy Poodles. This exceptionally intelligent breed can be taught many, many tricks and makes great companions for elderly women and single women who will not be sharing a home with children. Miniature and Standard Poodles do very well with children, who will love teaching them tricks. They are protective and will alert you if your child is getting into trouble. They are very playful yet are agile enough not to knock into small children.

People either think Poodles are the most stunning of all dogs, or depending on the Poodle's "hairstyle," they will think she is the funniest looking dog they have ever seen. Definitely a favorite among the rich, Poodles, especially Standard Poodles, are adored by those sharp enough to realize that this is one breed whose looks can be quite deceiving. Women, of course, are immediately attracted to their beauty, brains, and charisma. Men who are very comfortable with their masculinity and not worried about "what the guys will say" love cohabitating with these dogs.

Of the all toy dogs, the **Pug** is the breed least suited to children. They are sturdier than most other small dogs, but they have protruding eyes that are very susceptible to injury, debris, or even a loss of an eyeball. Rough children can seriously hurt the Pug.

Amiable little dogs, Pugs are happy to meet and greet everyone they see and make great therapy dogs.

Silky Terriers and **Yorkshire Terriers** are both scrappy breeds given that they were bred to be ratters. They make excellent companions for a single woman living in the country or the city. Children can irritate these little dogs, so this is a combination I strongly advise against. They will bark when someone is around alerting you to any creeps, and they are affectionate and love to cuddle in bed. Who needs a partner when you can share your bed with a dog?

These are two more breeds that really like to bark hello, even before they come close enough to physically greet you. Women admire their spunkiness and men really appreciate their character.

The Melting Pot Dogs

Melting pot dogs are also known to the AKC as non-sporting dogs. They are dogs that really don't fit into any other group so they are relegated to the non-sporting group. They are sometimes considered the "red-headed stepchild" group of dogs.

The **Bichon Frise** is a bright and friendly little dog. Their propensity to bark makes them good watchdogs. Children are good with these dogs provided they are taught to understand and respect that sometimes these dogs want to be left alone and that they are not big dogs with a lot of tolerance for rough play. They are great for women who live alone.

This dog will no doubt introduce you to everyone. With the beauty of a Poodle, the charm of a toy, and the confidence level of a terrier, your Bichon Frise will attract everyone who loves dogs. You don't need to worry if you are shy. Just let her lead the way and she will let everyone know that you have both arrived.

Excellent barkers, **Boston Terriers** are great watchdogs, and owners of all kinds enjoy their low grooming needs. Be cautious of them with children, as rowdy ones can really harm these devilish but lovable dogs, especially around their eyes.

Bulldogs are great, largish dogs in not very little packages. They have low endurance so don't take them running, but they can tolerate moderate rough play with children. They are not good watchdogs since they are not known for barking, which makes them great for apartment living.

This is one dog that tough types love. Bulldogs have such personality that every manly man knows that these dogs rock. They also roll when they walk and don't forget the drool. You will definitely know if you have met someone who doesn't appreciate the beauty of a drool stain on her black pants once your Bulldog says hello. For those who miss having a man around the house, Bulldogs are the perfect substitute as they are great at lying around snoring, snorting, and farting.

The **Dalmatian** is another victim of irresponsibility and lack of knowledge. Dalmatians have become popular due to *101 Dalmatians* but are not necessarily good for children due to their size and strength. Unfortunately, due to the popularity of the Disney movie, many children see the adorable polka-dotted puppies and want one. To appease their children, parents buy one without having any knowledge of the breed's temperament. *The Dalmatian is a very active and strong-willed breed.* If you are a woman with children, do yourself a favor and pick a different breed. Your plate is full enough taking care of your family without adding an overly active dog to the mix.

Dalmatians will bring any child running and you will certainly never have anyone ask you what kind of dog you have. Not overly friendly, a Dalmatian will give you something to talk about, but don't expect her to drag you over to a stranger so that you can start a conversation.

The **French Bulldog** is another dog that has earned a special place in my heart. I first worked with one in 1979. Black and Decker contacted my dad to do a commercial with Dallas Cowboy Bob Lilly. They wanted a Bulldog to spring out of a doghouse that Bob had built with his Black and Decker tools. The doghouse had already been built and was not big enough to accommodate a Bulldog. When my dad spoke to them, he recommended a French Bulldog, a dog about half the size of a Bulldog with tons of spunk and tolerant of rough play with big dogs and children. The day of the shoot the dog wouldn't "spring" out of the doghouse. They had to stop filming and cut a hole in the back of the doghouse so someone could hold the gorgeous brindle Frenchie (owned by the late Mr. and Mrs. Bob Griffin) from behind and release her at the right moment getting her to "spring" out of the doghouse. There was only one person on the set small enough who could do that job: me! That was my very first theatrical job with dogs. To this day, I am not sure if my dad ever paid me, but he does tell me all the time if it hadn't been for me the commercial would never have been made.

Ah, the **Poodle**! I fussed over the Toy Poodle in the last section, and I get to do it again with the **Standard** and **Miniature** Poodle. Again, this is a superb breed, no matter the size. I have heard them often referred to as the Labrador with a Ph.D. because of their absolute brilliance. I believe this to be the most intelligent of all breeds capable of being trained to do just about anything and everything. You can give your Poodle this book and in about a half hour the training will be completed. Poodles make excellent watchdogs, are wonderful with children (although young children are not suitable for Toys), and just love people and learning. The only potential drawback is the frequent and expensive visits to the spa.

Before you even think about getting a Poodle, make sure you will always be able to allow for grooming fees in your budget no matter what happens in your life. I can guarantee you one thing—this is one breed that is not "do-it-yourself."

The **Shiba Inu** is a great dog for people who live in apartments and want a quiet dog. Like cats, these dogs are not as eager to please as other breeds and do not care to be a big playmate for children, unless it means they can play chase. Single, quiet women do well with the Shiba Inu, as long as they don't allow the Shiba to take over the house.

I have noticed that people who are quiet and neat really enjoy meeting the Shiba. Be aware, however, that this is not a breed that will introduce you to anyone. You will have to introduce yourself.

Have You Herd?

Bright, determined, and active, herding dogs are comfortable in an apartment, park, farm, or any other place you may live.

The **Australian Cattle Dog** is a bit aloof, a good watchdog, and a fan of exercise. If you have a teenaged boy, he would be good company for a Cattle Dog. The Cattle Dog is a smallish, strong, compact dog that would enjoy going to the park or running alongside a bicycle.

Sort of an unknown dog, your Cattle Dog will attract curious passersby who will ask what kind of dog she is. Since Cattle Dogs are athletic, they are great to bring to the jogging trail to meet people who like to stay fit and keep active. This is one breed that will attract anything from a truck driver to an attorney, a surfer dude to a college professor.

Australian Shepherds are affectionately known as Aussies. Aussies started to gain popularity in the United States in the early 1990s after they were entered into the *AKC Stud Book* in 1991 and the herding group in 1993.

The first Australian Shepherd I trained was in the summer of 1986. Blythe was a black and white dog and she was in training for guide dog work. She was actually the first Aussie trained for this type of work in the United States. Aussies are very sweet dogs with a happy disposition. They do well with children who aren't rough, provided they have been bred, socialized, and trained properly. Aussies need to be trained early, and, as with all dogs, kept in a fenced-in yard or on a leash when outside, so they don't take up car herding.

The Australian Shepherd is a friendly, approachable breed. If you are very shy, don't hesitate to teach your Aussie some tricks. You can then "just practice" in front of the person you would like to start talking to and he or she will most likely start up a conversation. I have seen all types of people go for Aussies—doctors, lawyers, truck drivers, and college students.

Bearded Collies are wonderful family companions. They are sweet and enjoy training. They are happiest playing with gentle children or sharing a home with a single woman who will spend time brushing their coat and exercising them regularly. They learn tricks easily too.

Most people will mistake your Bearded Collie for an Old English Sheepdog. Due to her very amiable personality, she will probably be happy to introduce you to anyone you want.

The three **Belgian** breeds include the **Malinois**, **Sheepdog**, and the **Tervuren**. These are very bright dogs; however, it is imperative that you don't have one as your very first dog. Very active dogs, they can be a bit of a handful for the first-time dog owner.

The rest of the world recognizes these dogs as the same breed, but the AKC does not. In 1959 the AKC separated them as distinct breeds. There is a slight difference in their temperaments. The Malinois is by far the most active of the three, and the Tervuren and the Sheepdog have higher grooming requirements due to their long plush coats.

They are known to be handler-protective as opposed to area-protective like the German Shepherd. These are not breeds I recommend for anyone with small children. I have owned and shown them, some even to their championships. I have also done a bit of rescue work for the Malinois and have shared my home with many.

WHAT IS "AREA-PROTECTIVE" AND "HANDLER-PROTECTIVE"?

Dogs that are area-protective, such as the German Shepherd, will protect your home and property by constantly patrolling the area, whereas a handler-protective dog, such as a Malinois, will stay by your side. A perpetrator may jump the fence, but he is not coming near you without having all of his limbs ripped off and being devoured by your Malinois.

Next time you watch the news and see clips of bomb or drug dogs, take a close look. That may not be a German Shepherd that you see, but a Malinois.

At the end of President Clinton's presidency, there was a great picture of him on the front page of the *New York Times* with a Malinois who had found a very large shipment of cocaine.

The Malinois is one breed men will go gaga over. These dogs excel in protection sports such as SchutzHund and Ring Sport, often putting the longtime participant German Shepherd to shame. If status is important to you, think twice about a Malinois. I would often walk down the street with one of my champion Belgian Malinois, and people would innocently ask, "Shepherd mix?"

Border Collies have received quite a bit of attention since it was announced that they are the most intelligent of all breeds. While I believe they are highly intelligent, I don't believe they are the smartest of all dogs. They do well in obedience, agility, and herding competition as well as other dog sports. I don't recommend them for a family unless you plan on spending a lot of time training and competing in a dog sport with the dog. Border Collies are great dogs, but they need to be kept busy; otherwise, they will become destructive. You may have children and think it would be great for them to become active in agility competition, but training requires a large time commitment. I would encourage you not to get a Border Collie until you have had another kind of dog first and your child has shown a huge commitment to learning the sport of agility, obedience, fly ball, or any other dog sport. When competing you must practice daily, go to training weekly, and travel on the weekends, which is not just a large time commitment but a financial one as well. Competing is a very rewarding hobby but also demanding. Border Collies are not dogs to greet you when you come home and then lie at your feet watching television.

Everyone will recognize your dog. They will tell you how she is supposed to be the smartest of all breeds. I believe she is just another willing workaholic.

Bouvier des Flandres is a very strong-willed dog. They do require a bit of grooming and are great dogs for protecting your home. They can physically and mentally put up with a lot of abuse from children, but it is important they learn at an early age that they are not in charge.

They are not very common so be prepared; many people will ask you about them. Men will also like them because they are big and strong "real dogs." Do men always have to think size is everything? Jeez. Due to the tenacity and strength of these dogs do not expect introverts or small children to want to run up and pet your Bouvier.

Collies are soft, gentle dogs that require gentle, quiet older children and a lady who is willing to groom them daily. Children and adults alike will love to say hello to your Lassie.

Good old Rin Tin Tin. We are all familiar with the **German Shepherd Dog** hero. Many grew up with them. This is the kind of dog that will greet you with a kiss, attack the burglar, and drag you from a burning building risking her life. Unfortunately, these dogs have fallen out of popularity due to bad press, irresponsible ownership, and poor breeding. The most common reason I hear people say for not wanting a German Shepherd Dog is "because of the hips." If you go to a breeder

THE ORTHOPEDIC FOUNDATION FOR ANIMALS

It is important to remember that many breeds have a predisposition to hip dysplasia. If you are considering one of these breeds, make sure you see the certificates on both parents that state Orthopedic Foundation for Animals (OFA). If these certificates are not made available to you, you can check the ratings on the OFA's website at offa.org using the registered names of the parents. The information on the website is deemed very reliable.

If you are unsure about your chosen breed's propensity toward hip dysplasia, you can access that information from the American Kennel Club at akc.org.

who is responsible and has all breeding stock certified by the Orthopedic Foundation for Animals (OFA), chances are you will greatly decrease the risk of getting a dog with bad hips.

One of two things will happen when people see you walking down the street. They will turn and go the other way, or they will stop and tell you about the German Shepherd they had as a kid.

The **Shetland Sheepdog**, affectionately known as the Sheltie, is a wonderful breed. I call this miniature Collie genetically obedient. This is one breed of dog that doesn't need extensive training for the average dog owner. The only complaints trainers get with Shelties is that they bark a lot, which makes them terrific watchdogs. Just don't let the burglar see the gentle, cute fur ball bouncing up and down as she barks and runs in circles at the ringing doorbell. They are great with children and wonderful for women, young, old, quiet, or outgoing.

Shelties are very sweet dogs but not outgoing; it will be up to you to make a new friend. Often you can depend on your Sheltie to bark hello, but usually it is not a welcoming gesture as much as it is to alert you. Young children, especially girls, love Shelties. Women will certainly admire your Sheltie's beauty.

It is interesting to note that loyal German Shepherd Dog fanciers will invariably own a **Welsh Corgi**—either the **Cardigan** or the **Pembroke**—as their "other" breed. You will find them a favorite among the horsey set as well. They make great watchdogs. Since they are big dogs in dwarfed packages, they can do well in either an apartment or on a farm. They don't need frequent visits to the dog salon, they are easy to train, and they will be great companions for those who may be older and live alone or for young families with children who know how to be kind and gentle around dogs.

Corgis are loved by all kinds of women, and men appreciate these big dogs that come in little packages. Corgis will run around and around. Everyone will laugh at their unbelievable speed for such little legs.

Using Your Dog as an Icebreaker

You have carefully read through this whole chapter, and you really want a dog. You may also really want to make some new friends or find a partner but just do not feel completely comfortable making the first move. A dog can help you break the ice . . .

The breed that you want is not an overly friendly dog nor is it a breed that will attract the person you have your eyes on. Get the dog that is right for you. I am going to tell you how to use your new puppy as an icebreaker to meet the people you think you would like to get to know better.

They have seen your dog, but they haven't made the first move to say hello. One of two things could be happening here. One: they don't like dogs. Or two: they are shy themselves. Well, if they don't like dogs, you probably won't like them anyway so . . . And if they are shy or feeling a bit socially inept, here are a few tried-and-true lines and approaches:

First let's find out if they like dogs:

1. You are at the mailbox. Accidentally and oh so subtly drop a treat near their foot. If they kick your dog, you know they are not someone you want to befriend. If they don't notice, they probably don't mind dogs one bit.

Yet, you still haven't gotten them to start a conversation so what next? Here are a few lines:

2. "Hey, do you have a dog?" If they answer yes, say, "Maybe our dogs could get together to play."
3. If they answer, "No, I don't have a dog," ask incredulously, "Really?" Now, if they don't like dogs, they will simply confirm what they just told you and continue to look through their mail.
4. If they say no but they really like dogs or have had a dog, they will start telling you about their past dog or why they don't have a dog now.
5. You can also assume that they have a dog and say, "Hey, who is your veterinarian?" If they tell you that they don't have one, you can just write it off and say, "Oh, I am just looking for one for my dog."
6. Another line is (and this one will separate the dog lovers from the ones to cross off your potential friend list), "I am going to be away over the weekend. Do you know anyone who might be willing to watch my puppy?" If they say they will, then you are in luck. Oh yeah—you aren't really going away. Just call them the day before and say, "Hey, my plans were changed for the weekend. Thanks, but I won't need for you to watch Sammy, but I owe you one. Do you want to go to the dog park/see a movie/grab a coffee with me?" Their answer doesn't matter here—they may already have plans. You have broken the ice and found a person to watch your dog for you when you go away. A little warning here: if this is a guy and you

have a habit of falling for guys who end up on "America's Most Wanted" or "Cops," you may want to reassess whether you really want him watching Sammy. But if he reminds you of Richie Cunningham, then by all means, let him watch her.

OK, so none of these ideas has worked just yet. I am going to give you an even better idea. Buy the book *How to Teach Your Dog to Talk*. It has more than two hundred tricks in there. It is truly an amazing training book! Buy a hat and find a place in town where all the tourists or drunken college students converge. Go to that location and start your trick dog show. Send your dog around the crowd carrying the hat for the onlookers to drop in money. Even if you meet no one, you will be able to pay the rent.

"Hey, Babette! Isn't that your dad's book?" you ask. Of course, it is. I am an only child. My parents are divorced. Who do you think will get the royalties when he dies? If I recommended someone else's book, it wouldn't be wise financial planning.

Safety Issues

If you stay in the safety zone all the
time, you'll never know about your
strength. You'll never know yourself at
your most brilliant.

—Bernice Johnson Regon

No dog book (training or general) is ever complete without a discussion on safety issues. Your dog's safety is really the primary reason to train your dog. At the very least you want your dog to know her name and answer to it. Why? 'Cause you are a control freak who gets off on bossing your dog around? No. It's for safety's sake. You may need to call her away from a busy street or see her getting something into her mouth, and you want her to be trained to respond to you. There is nothing better than a well-behaved dog, but just remember that the commands I teach in this book are first and foremost for your dog's safety. Please note that some of the commands we'll be using in this chapter are discussed in greater detail in Part 2. Refer to the Contents or Index for specific commands.

Emergency Situations

You never know when you will find yourself in an emergency situation with your dog. Perhaps your dog gets hit by a car, is bitten by another dog, or is somehow injured during a natural or man-made disaster. You may not be able to take your dog to the vet and will instead have to rely on yourself and others to help your dog. For instance, many of my South Florida clients know that in the event of a tropical storm, like Hurricane Andrew back in 1992, they may need their neighbors to help them perform some sort of procedure on their dog, such as putting a splint on a broken leg. In such a situation your dog will already be highly stressed. Having a kind stranger or neighbor helping you will likely increase your dog's stress level and the propensity to bite. For everyone's safety you will want to muzzle your dog; however, you may not have a muzzle on hand, but if you have a leash, you can make what is called a hasty muzzle.

The Hasty Muzzle

The hasty muzzle is an important trick that originated in the military. Soldiers learned they could muzzle their dogs without carrying a muzzle. Soldiers can't carry too much gear and may be in a situation, such as in the middle of a swamp, in which they need to muzzle their dogs without a muzzle, hence, the hasty muzzle. It is called "hasty" because it is something you have to do quickly. Even if you are not a soldier, there may be a time when you need to quickly muzzle your dog:

1. Stand with Isabella in the sit position on your left side.
2. Use your left hand and take a six-foot leash at its snap. Say, "Muzzle it."
3. With your right hand, take the free end of the leash and run the leash under her muzzle.
4. Holding the leash in your right hand wrap it over the muzzle two times.
5. Bring the leash around and behind Isabella's neck.
6. At the back of Isabella's neck snugly hold together with your left hand.

Place the leash under her muzzle.
Photo by www.mortonimages.com.

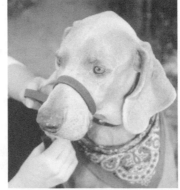

I wrap the leash over the muzzle snugly but not too tight. Photo by www.mortonimages.com.

Two times over the muzzle. Photo by www.mortonimages.com.

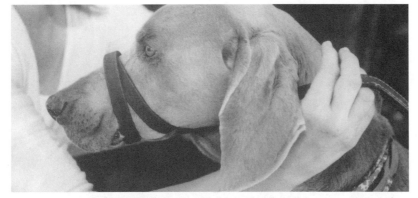

Taking the end of the leash, I bring it high up behind Isabella's ears on top of her head and hold it snugly. Photo by www.mortonimages.com.

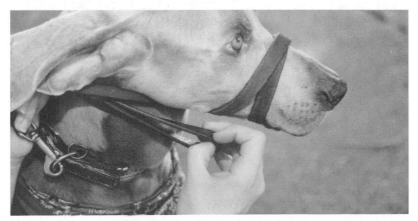

We now have a safe and snug hold on her head. Photo by www.mortonimages.com.

If you don't have a leash available, you can tie her muzzle closed with a belt or a piece of rope. You would simply wrap it around her muzzle and tie it. Be sure that it is not too tight so that you can remove it with ease.

The Homemade Stretcher

Perhaps your dog gets injured or takes ill and you need to rush her to the veterinarian. She cannot walk and you cannot lift her ninety-pound body. Many times we further injure our dogs by moving them, but somehow we have to move them in order to get them the help they need. Follow these steps to make and use a homemade stretcher in order to transport them as safely as possible:

1. What you want to do is put your dog in the down position. When she is lying down, make sure she is on her side, an advantage to the "on your back" position introduced in Chapter 8.
2. Lay a flat piece of cardboard or plywood next to her, trying to place the board underneath her back as much as possible. Take her by the legs that are closest to the ground and carefully flip her so that she is completely on the board. If she is still close to the edge, you can slide her closer to the center. Carefully slide her to your vehicle. If you don't have a board, you can use a sheet instead as shown in

Jolie lies next to the sheet. Photo by Liz Mayer.

A well-trained Jolie completely trusts me as she toler-ates this turning over. Photo by Liz Mayer.

Jolie learned through obedience that she can trust me and she will allow me to help her in an emergency. Photo by Liz Mayer.

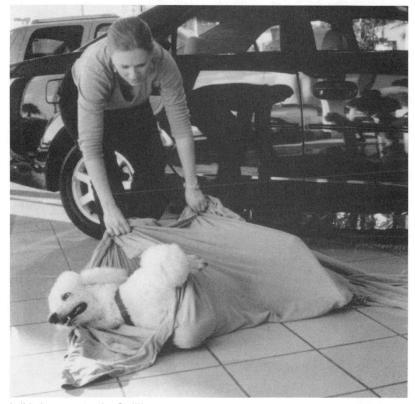

I slide her over to the Cadillac. Photo by Liz Mayer.

As I kneel down, I say, "Relax, Jolie." Photo by Liz Mayer.

the photos. Gently roll her over onto the sheet and slide her to the car.

3. Now picking her up and placing her into the car will be difficult for you. If you have an SUV or minivan, it will be easier for you to put her in the rear. There are two ways to get her into the car from the homemade stretcher. If you have something, such as another piece of plywood, lay it as a ramp into the vehicle. Get behind it or above it and slide it into the vehicle. Or you can take the stretcher, place it "ramp style" to the vehicle, go to the bottom, and push up.

4. If you don't have anything to use as a ramp, you will need to lift her. If you need to lift her, there is a way to do this, very carefully. First say out loud: "I am going to lift you with ease and get you in this car." Close your eyes and picture yourself lifting her. Kneel down and slide both forearms as far under her as possible Take a deep breath, count to three, and then on three, lift, and roll her toward you as you exhale and lift *quickly*. There are two important things here— rolling her toward you so that she lies in the crook of your arms and lifting quickly because you don't have time to think about what is happening.

I tell her, "I will lift all sixty pounds of you." Photo by Liz Mayer.

We did it! Let's get you to the vet!
Photo by Liz Mayer.

Home Safety

Just as you would childproof your home for a baby, you should do
the same for your puppy. The house has all sorts of temptations for
curious dogs.

Your Puppy's Crate

This first tip is for the safety of both your dog and any children in
your home. In our home we always place a safety clip on the door
of our dog's crate. Children at young ages can open up a crate; however, if you have added some extra hidden clips, they may not realize right away why the door is not opening. Be certain that the
children don't see how you are opening and closing the crate door
or how you are using the clips. This will stop them from letting the
dog out, or even worse, bothering the dog while she is eating. Most
dog bites come from the family dog, not the rotten mean dog down
the street. These bites are most often in the face, so beware!

Poisons

Poisons such as household cleaners, antifreeze, bleach, bug killers,
mothballs, and rat and mouse repellants are always a danger if they
are not stored safely away. Don't fall into a sense of false security
and think your dog won't like the smell of something so she won't

drink it. What you may find displeasing, she may find quite yummy. Make sure you keep all cleaners and potentially hazardous items locked up. I would recommend not using the type of cleanser in your toilet that exists between flushes. If your girl drinks it, she may die. If you need to use a cleanser or a freshener in your toilet, get a lock for the seat lid. I have known dogs that will stick their heads under the closed lid just to get a drink. You can get these toilet lid locks in a hardware or baby supply store.

Personal Care Products

The same is true of personal care products, such as shampoo and deodorant, the smells and tastes of which your dog may find pleasing. These contain all sorts of chemicals that could kill your girl if she were to ingest them.

Material Hazards

Just like children, dogs find the strangest things interesting and tasty. Take care to always put away items your dog might decide to eat, which in turn could create a blockage and cause your dog to need surgery. For example, you want to make sure that you don't leave any of your panties or stockings lying around. If your dog ingests either, that could make a very expensive trip to Victoria's Secret. Be especially aware after you wear them. Make sure to put them into the hamper. The odors and fluids we emit smell and taste yummy to dogs, so they are more likely to eat our underwear or nylons after we wear them.

Other items you don't want lying around include plastic bags, dry cleaning bags, sandwich bags, bubble wrap, and packing "popcorn."

Those are the obvious ones, and then there are the less obvious ones. I remember a Bull Terrier that I trained in New York. This dog grabbed his owner's 2.5-carat engagement ring and promptly swallowed it in front of her. The owner was in the process of deciding whether she wanted to marry this guy or not, and I think that her dog was trying to tell her something. Neither the dog nor I liked this guy, and the poor dog needed surgery to get the ring back. The dog fortunately recovered.

Chocolate and Other Food

Chocolate. Every girl loves chocolate. I remember a college friend's theory that the only people who didn't like chocolate were those who didn't like sex. I am not sure if she ever proved it. Your dog will also love chocolate, but it will kill her. Chocolate has theobromine, which can't be processed by a dog's liver. Your dog will die very quickly. If you think she may have ingested chocolate, give her one teaspoon of hydrogen peroxide per ten pounds of body weight. Bring her outside and wait for her to vomit. While waiting, you can call your veterinarian.

You also want to avoid giving your dog pork, onions, pineapple, and avocado—all foods that can be poisonous to dogs.

BELIEVE IT OR NOT!

A plastic surgeon told me the story of one of his patients. One New Year's Eve, she came home drunker than a skunk. When she went to give her Akita a hug and kiss, he nearly ripped her face off. If you have been out saucing it up with the girls, be careful how you approach your dog. The smell of alcohol, your not walking in a straight line, as well as your unusual behavior can be confusing for your best friend.

Things That Can Electrocute or Cut

You will want to crawl around and make sure that all wires and outlets are hidden and all breakables are secure—not just from her mouth but from her tail as well. You might consider sectioning off potential danger areas with a baby gate.

Plants and Other Dangers in the Yard

Rosie was a great Rottweiler that I trained about ten years ago. The owner was landscaping her spacious property. She bought a particular plant that according to the information from the nursery was a nontoxic plant. Rosie ate the plant, had a seizure, and almost died. Rosie's owner found out that in large quantities the plant was very toxic.

Before you landscape or bring home a new plant, contact the veterinary school in your state or region and ask about the toxicity of any plants you are considering. Veterinary schools are a great resource for this type of information. They also maintain databases on toxic plants indigenous to your region. You will also learn that your local veterinary school has terrific databases of useful information about caring for your dog and diseases that are common in your area.

In the yard, you want to make sure all fertilizers and weed killers are securely sealed. Also remember that if you treat your yard with seeds or pesticides, your dog may eat the grass after a fresh application. Be sure that anything you spray is good and dry before you let your dog outside.

One day I was at the office of my vet, Dr. Berkenblit. Dr. B received an emergency call from a man who had been using his weed whacker and his dog ran into it. She was cut up pretty badly on her legs, but, fortunately, she was going to be fine. You should never ever let your dog be near you when you are operating any type of machinery in the yard, garage, or house.

Swimming Pools and Ponds

Never allow your dog to stay by a pool or pond unattended. I know of two dogs whose owners left them out by their pool and both dogs drowned. One family wasn't sure if the young dog fell in while playing with the other dogs and couldn't get out or what really happened. They just found her at the bottom of the pool. Another had an older, blind and arthritic dog. The dog must have fallen in and couldn't get out either.

Make sure your dog knows how to get out of the pool, but don't count on that to save her. She could fall in and panic.

Traveling by Car

My first recommendation for safely traveling in the car with your dog is to make sure she is secure by using a crate, harness, seatbelt, or leash. If you are in a car accident, your dog will not become a flying object, injuring herself, you, and the other passengers in the car. I remember a car accident involving a woman and her dog on the highway that occurred a few years ago. The owner was injured and couldn't get out of the car. Her dog had not been properly secured and ran all over the highway until someone was able to catch him.

Case in Point

About six years ago I was working with two Welsh Springer Spaniels. They were two great littermates, a male and female. As is typical of the breed, they were very active. One Monday morning Steve and Mary told us how they had a wonderful trip to their home in Northern Florida for some relaxation; however, they'd had a harrowing experience on the drive up. They admitted they hadn't heeded my advice to put the dogs in crates while traveling by car. When they stopped at a rest area to let the dogs relieve themselves, both dogs jumped out of the car before Steve and Mary could put the leashes on them. The dogs took off. Fortunately for Torrey and Harley, a trucker was able to stop his eighteen-wheeler, get out, and catch the friendly dogs.

Crates

Invest in an airline crate just big enough for her to turn around in and lie down. It doesn't need to be as big as her crate at home, just enough room for comfort. Buy a grid to fit on the bottom of the crate so that if there is an accident or your dog vomits, she will still stay dry, or you can place a towel in with her, which will keep her comfortable especially if she salivates profusely in the car.

When traveling by car, it is wise to put your dog in the crate wearing a leash. When you get to a rest stop, you will already have a leash on her. This will decrease the chance of her jumping out of the crate, becoming startled, and running around the rest area.

It is also very important to teach your dog not to burst out of her crate. Remember when opening the crate or car door, you must first tell her to stay. Do not open the door until she sits and stays. Some dogs are very excited at the prospect of getting out of the crate to enjoy all of the new smells. The following is a very simple and fast way to stop her from running out of the crate door:

1. Unclip and start opening the crate door.
2. As she starts to burst out, close the door.
3. Wait a moment. Tell her to stay.
4. Slowly open the door again.

A WORD ON CRATES

I prefer the airline crates over the metal crates. They are quieter, easy to clean, and most importantly, if you have to travel by plane, you already have the type of crate the airline requires. Before you think, "Oh I would never fly with her," pretend you live in South Florida and a hurricane is coming that is bigger than the state. You need to leave *now*, not later.

In a disaster, an airline crate will offer your dog the best protection. For example, if an object, such as a shard of glass, comes flying at your dog's crate, chances are the glass will break and shatter into a metal crate, whereas an airline crate will better prevent the glass from getting inside and cutting your dog.

Even if Mother Nature is quiet where you live, an airline crate provides a dark, cozy, den-like environment that dogs crave.

5. When she starts to push her way out, tell her no.
6. Close the door.
7. Repeat.

By the third time you practice this procedure, she will learn that she must wait until you are ready for her to come out of the crate. It is best if you teach her this at home. It takes less than five minutes and the results can save her life.

Harness, Seatbelt, or Leash

If putting your dog in a crate is not an option for you, then I suggest purchasing a harness or dog seatbelt; however, it has been my experience that dogs can figure out how to get out of both of these.

If you are using a harness, you will take it and put it on your dog, according to the product's directions—don't forget her collar so that when you arrive at your destination, you can walk as usual. Once you put the harness on your dog, you will put her in the right rear seat of your vehicle. This is the best place for two reasons: (1) being in the front seat could kill your dog if the air bag goes off, and (2) if you want to check on your dog, you will be able to see the right rear through the rearview mirror whereas you would need to turn around to see the left rear. If you only have a hatchback or two-door car, the safest place is still the back seat; otherwise, she could go through the windshield if the air bag doesn't kill her first.

If you are using a seatbelt, be sure to install it in the right rear seat and secure your dog inside, following the manufacturer's directions exactly.

A third option for securing your dog inside a car is using her leash and securing it within the car door. Even if you have your dog secured in a harness or seatbelt, you may choose to be extra safe by also doing the following.

CUTE STORY

Last year for my birthday my husband made a card for me. Since he has promised to buy me a blue Porsche Cabriolet for my fortieth birthday, which is in a few years, he took a picture of one and put me in the driver's seat along with my German Shepherd Barkley next to me. Before he gave it to me (the card, not the car, unfortunately), he realized it wasn't a good idea for Barkley to be in the front seat so he redid it. We both looked hipper in the front seat, but Barkley is safer in the back.

Have your dog hop in on the right rear seat wearing her collar with the leash attached to it. Making sure to allow enough slack for her to sit or lie down comfortably, take the end of the leash and close the car door on it, so that the end of the leash is sticking outside. This way you will have control over your dog when you open the door again, stopping her from running into traffic. This also prevents her from jumping into your lap or obstructing your view while you are driving. And finally, restraining her in this manner will stop her from flying through the window or slamming into you, possibly killing you both, if you are involved in an accident.

GETTING YOUR DOG IN AND OUT OF THE CAR

1. Place your dog in a sit-stay before you open the car door.
2. Open the door and tell her to get into the car.
3. Give her enough leash to sit or lie down and to turn around but not an excessive amount.
4. Place half of the leash in the door frame (see photos on next page).
5. Close the door. (When you arrive at your destination, you will be able to control your dog, so she cannot jump out and run away.)
6. When you reach your destination, tell your dog to stay first. Grasp the leash and place your leg in front of the door so she can't push it open.
7. Hold on to the leash and slowly open the door. Don't allow your dog to jump out. Block her way until it is safe and then call her to you.

Jolie and Louie are sitting and waiting for me to open the car door. Photo by Liz Mayer.

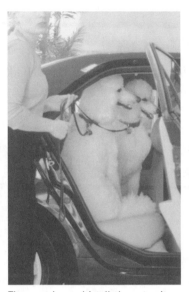

They get in, and I tell them to sit and stay. Photo by Liz Mayer.

I make sure that there is enough leash but not so much that they have room to move around in the car. Photo by Liz Mayer.

Telling them to stay, I hold half of the leash and close the door on it. Photo by Liz Mayer.

When I open the door, I grab the leash, so they aren't able to jump out and run off in excitement. Photo by Liz Mayer.

We are here! I grasp the leash and place my leg in front of the door so that they can't push it open. Photo by Liz Mayer.

Still grasping the leash, I slowly open the door, keeping them calm. Photo by Liz Mayer.

I don't allow them to run out. I block their way out, telling them to stay first. Photo by Liz Mayer.

I call them to me. They are calm and under control. Photo by Liz Mayer.

Car Windows

If you have power windows, make sure you keep the lock on the window so your dog can't open or close the window and risk an injury. About eight years ago, one of our trainers had to pick up two dogs for training. She put the Lab puppy in the car, securing him in to the seat. Leaving the car running she ran back into the house to get the Yorkie. In the Lab's excitement he scratched at the window and locked the doors. I received the early morning call; she didn't have an extra set of keys. While I drove to give her a set of keys, the dog sat and listened to Howard Stern in the nice air-conditioned car. The not so funny part was that her car was blocking the garage, and the owner was a doctor who had to get to work but was blocked. Fortunately, there were no emergencies that morning. Learn from her mistakes. Don't ever leave your dog unattended in the car, and when riding together, always activate the child safety features.

I am not sure why people of seeming above average intelligence insist on allowing their dogs to stick their heads out of the window while driving. Doing so puts your dog's eyes at risk because dirt, debris, insects, and other flying objects can get in the eyes and destroy them. Don't allow her to stick her head out the window. You will save her eyes and keep your veterinary bills down.

Door Safety

It happens again and again. People open a door and their dogs rush past them, out the door, and into the street where they are hit by a car. If the owners had placed their dogs in a sit-stay or had been holding them by their leash, they may have been able to avoid such a tragedy. Just getting through a door with your dog can be a challenge. It will be even more difficult if you have children in tow or are pushing a carriage. There are many types of doors that you may encounter with your dog:

- doors that open in toward you
- doors that open out away from you

- sliding glass doors
- revolving doors
- swinging doors—either in or out

Now there are several ways to get through each of these doors safely. In each situation you should be holding your dog on a leash the entire time.

A door that opens toward or away from you is pretty simple. As a rule whenever you come to a door, place your dog in a sit-stay *before* opening the door. Once you open the door, heel her through the door. As soon as you get on the other side, put her in a sit-stay again and then turn to close the door.

With a sliding glass door you can do the same thing. Another option is to place your dog in a sit-stay while you walk out the door holding on to her leash. Once you are through the door, you can then call your dog to you and have her sit while you close the door.

Revolving doors can be somewhat tricky. You may need to place your dog on your right side where it is wider giving her more room to move.

When going through a swinging door, make sure you hold it open for your dog so she doesn't get smacked in the rear or in the face by the door.

If you have a stroller with you, you may be better off placing your dog in a sit-stay before going through most doors. Then you go ahead with the stroller and once you are through the door, without having dropped the leash, you can then call her to you. If you are in a busy area, put her in a down-stay instead of the sit-stay to decrease the chances of her breaking her stay. Make sure that as you go through these doors, you do not drop the leash.

Stair Safety

Now you will have different situations for going up or down stairs with your dog, especially if you are carrying a child, a stroller, or groceries. You can do one of the following:

1. Place your dog in a down-stay.
2. Walk either up or down stairs.
3. Call her to you.

Or

1. Before going down or up the stairs, tell your dog to sit next to you.
2. As you start down or up the stairs, say, "Heel," and start walking together.
3. Once you get to the bottom or the top of the stairs, put her in a sit-stay.
4. Release and give lots of praise.

Elevator Safety

You have to be really careful when getting onto an elevator with your dog. While entering or exiting, do not take your eyes off of her and make sure her whole body, not just part of it, is clear from the door.

1. Place your dog in a sit-stay while you are waiting for the elevator to come.
2. Stick your arm out to keep the elevator from closing and walk together into the elevator.
3. Keep your arm in front of the door and your eyes on your dog.
4. Once you are both fully inside, place her in a sit-stay.
5. Follow this same procedure when exiting an elevator.

Going forward in this book, you will learn training techniques and commands that will assist you in keeping your dog safe. Don't be intimidated! They are easy and are the most basic tools. But don't confuse basic for "unimportant." These are actually the fundamental commands you will use as you increase your training expertise. If your dog can learn to sit, stay, move out of the way, come when called, drop it, go potty, and learn to love her crate, you will not only have a well-behaved, respectable, delightful companion, but a much safer dog.

I place Cali in a sit-stay while we wait for the elevator. Photo by Gordon Brennan.

I place my arm in front of the door to keep it from closing. Photo by Gordon Brennan.

Cali carefully heels into the elevator. I don't take my eyes off of her, making sure she is all the way inside the elevator. Photo by Gordon Brennan.

Sitting and staying happily in the elevator. Photo by Gordon Brennan.

TRAINING A DOG
THAT'S RIGHT FOR YOU

Getting Started with the Right Equipment

God does not ask for your ability or your
inability. He asks only for your
availability.

—Mary Kay Ash

When Suzanne hired us to train her one-year-old Great Dane, she told us of her trip to her first puppy class offered by another school. She was dragged into her class by her horse-sized Great Dane, Missy. The instructor brought Missy over to be fitted for a Halti. Suzanne laughed and said, "Do you have a prong collar?" The instructor's reply was, "They are not illegal but . . . "

There is nothing in the dog-training world that brings as much pandemonium and debate as when it comes to equipment. There are many pieces of equipment, some of which have been proven with the test of time to be excellent training tools. Still others are good management tools. There is a difference between a training tool and a management tool. The training tool is something that is used, a piece of equipment that changes or modifies a certain behavior, good, bad, or indifferent. The management tool is what you use until you are able to dedicate the time necessary for training.

CASE IN POINT

My friend loves to cook. She has a beautiful set of top-notch Wusthof knives. One day her husband was trying to break some ice in the bucket—by using an $80 Wusthof knife. He did effectively break the ice but he used the tool (knife) incorrectly and consequently broke the knife. Therefore, at the expense of using a very good tool incorrectly, he did get the results that he wanted—broken ice—but also results he didn't want—an upset wife and a very expensive but broken knife.

It is important to understand that any tool can be used effectively and correctly and any tool can also be used ineffectively and incorrectly. For example, let's say you want to put a hole in the wall to hang a picture. You could use a drill properly, and it will effectively give you a hole. Or, you can use a screwdriver, use it incorrectly by stabbing the wall with it, and not get the kind of hole you need.

As with child rearing and making your way up the corporate ladder, if plan A doesn't work, go to plan B, and so on. The same is true of dog training. If A, B, C don't work, try 1, 2, 3. Any good dog trainer

TRUE STORY

I remember a very nice girl named Ingrid who came to me for help with her Pit Bull. Her Pit Bull was about a year and a half. Ingrid had just moved to South Florida from Berkeley, California. As her Pit Bull dragged her into my school wearing a prong collar, the dog didn't even notice the prong collar digging into her neck. After doing a history profile on the dog, I found out she had gone to puppy class and the instructor had recommended a prong collar. I asked Ingrid if she had tried a training choker chain collar. Ingrid told me that the chain collar had no effect on her dog. I pointed out that the prong didn't either. We discussed the pros and cons and decided to go back to a training chain. After the training was completed, I suggested to Ingrid that she regularly switch collars without rhyme or reason. This way the dog wouldn't become immune to one particular collar and her own handling skills would stay sharp.

will have many tricks up her sleeve. The sooner the best trick is found, the better, because the sooner the problem is solved, the sooner you will be happy with your dog and your life less stressful. You may have no interest in training dogs; you just want yours to behave. It is important to keep in mind that there are many tools available to you. Don't be afraid to do something different.

Collars and Other Equipment

The following is not an all-inclusive list of collars and equipment, but the items listed are pieces you will want to learn how to use properly and they will all work for you and your dog. However, it is imperative to understand that with the exception of the flat buckle collar, your dog should wear these collars only when she is training and under your supervision. If you are not practicing, be sure to take the collar off of her.

- lightweight or medium-weight training choker chain collar
- fitted collar
- Martingale collar
- head halter
- prong collar
- citronella collar
- electronic collar
- vibrating collar
- five-foot leather leash—no wider than ¾ inch
- twenty-foot cotton web leash
- flat buckle collar
- treats

The **choker chain** is the safest collar to use on a dog because it is the one collar from which your dog cannot escape. I have seen dogs escape from every collar with the exception of the choker chain. When a choker chain is used properly, your dog will not feel dis-

Lightweight choker chain collar.
Photo by Gordon Brennan.

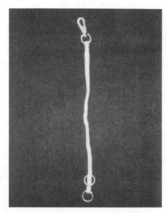

Fitted collar.
Photo by Gordon Brennan.

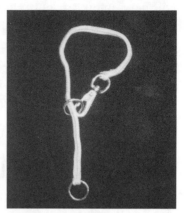

Fitted collar, snapped.
Photo by Gordon Brennan.

Martingale collar.
Photo by Gordon Brennan.

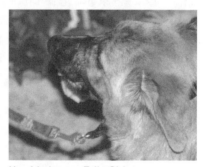

Head halter on Telly Girl.
Photo by Babette Haggerty-Brennan.

Prong collar. Photo by Gordon Brennan.

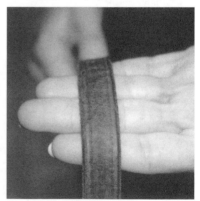

A ³/₄-inch-wide leather leash is so comfortable because it is no wider than the second phalange of my middle finger. Photo by Gordon Brennan.

comfort. Follow these steps to ensure you properly put the choker chain on your dog:

1. Take the collar and hold it with your left hand so that it hangs down vertically.
2. Take the bottom ring with your right hand.
3. Drop the chain into and through the bottom ring. Don't let go of it with your right hand.

This takes practice.

Photo by www.mortonimages.com.

Slowly place the links into the bottom ring. Photo by www.mortonimages.com.

You are almost there.

Photo by www.mortonimages.com.

Facing your dog, this is correct. You should read a proper *p*.

Photo by www.mortonimages.com.

Facing your dog, this is incorrect. You will read a backwards *p*.

Photo by www.mortonimages.com.

4. Bring your hands together and hold the chain with your right fingers. You will see that both rings are together.
5. Keeping both hands on the chain, turn it upside down.
6. Turn it around to make a proper *p*, not a backwards *p*.
7. Facing your dog, put the collar on as though *you* read the *p*, not your dog. She doesn't know how to spell yet.

The **fitted collar** has been called the Pearsall collar after Margaret and Milo Pearsall, and more recently the Volhard collar after trainers Jack and Wendy Volhard. The fitted collar sits high on a dog's neck, just below the ears. If you feel behind your dog's ears, you will feel a bit of a "valley," which is where the collar sits. It should fit snugly around her neck. You will first place the collar around your dog's neck and then snap it in place. To size it properly you must measure around your dog's neck at the "valley" and add one inch. As long as it is properly fastened, a fitted collar is nearly as safe as the choker chain. However, because the fitted collar sits high on your dog's neck, it works differently than a choker chain. Follow these steps to ensure you get a proper fit for your dog (please note that in the photos I am standing behind my dog so that you can see what I am doing; you will be facing your dog as you put the fitted collar on her following these steps):

1. Facing your dog, take the collar and place it around your dog's neck.
2. Make sure that the snap is on your right. The end ring should be on your left. The sliding ring should also be on your left.
3. Attach the snap to the sliding ring, not the end ring. There should be about one inch of excess collar.
4. Attach the leash to the end ring.

The **Martingale collar** has also been called a Greyhound collar. The advantage to this collar is that it doesn't break a dog's coat the way a chain collar can. If you have a dog that can be a bit frisky, putting this collar on in the beginning will be difficult. The collar is going to fit loosely over your dog's head, but once it is on her, you will then need to tighten it and size it appropriately. Follow these steps for a proper fit:

Lili patiently waits while I put a fitted collar on her.
Photo by Gordon Brennan.

Bringing the collar around her neck, it is high up and the snap is on your right as you face her.
Photo by Gordon Brennan.

The snap is attached to the sliding ring, high under her neck. Photo by Gordon Brennan.

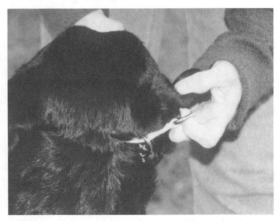

There should not be a lot of excess collar, only about one inch. Photo by Gordon Brennan.

The rings don't meet, showing that this Martingale collar fits correctly.
Photo by Gordon Brennan.

1. Take the collar and place it over your dog's head. And snap the collar.
2. Tighten the collar so that the two rings do not meet. If they do, the collar is too large.
3. Attach the leash to the top ring, which tightens the collar.

The **head halter** is a management tool. Of the various brand names available, I prefer the Comfort Trainer head halter. We will discuss the practical application of this tool in more detail as we move through the book. The downside is that brachycephalic dogs—dogs with short muzzles, such as Pugs and Boxers—have a difficult time wearing head halters. It does take quite some time for many dogs to accustom themselves to this type of collar because it can be exceptionally stressful. Follow these steps to ensure a proper fit:

With your left hand place the muzzle piece of the head halter on first.
Photo courtesy of Gordon Brennan.

Holding a treat in your right hand in front of the muzzle will force her to stick her nose through the muzzle to take the treat. Photo courtesy of Gordon Brennan.

Be sure to praise your dog as you feed her the treat. Photo courtesy of Gordon Brennan.

1. Purchase the appropriate size for your dog.
2. Have her sit in front of you.
3. With your left hand place the muzzle piece on first.
4. Hold a treat in the right hand in front of the muzzle—this will force her to stick her nose through the muzzle to take the treat.
5. As she chews on the treat, give her lots of praise.
6. Take the collar part of the halter and size and fit around her neck. Make sure that it sits high on her neck.

Your dog will most likely become stressed when first wearing this type of collar, and one of three things will happen when you put it on her: (1) She will buck like a bronco, which can be very dangerous. If your dog does that, stop and wait until she calms. (2) She will freeze in her tracks. (3) She will drop to her belly and not move. Be patient and don't pull on it. Try to offer her treats, but depending on her level of stress, she probably will not accept any. Use this collar with caution because dogs have been known to slip right out of them. If your dog is able to free herself, she will know if she tries hard enough she can always get out of it. This is a lesson you don't want her to learn, so always make sure to size the collar properly.

You may also find that when your dog is wearing one, people may think it is a muzzle, which causes them to fear your dog. Don't take it personally; just explain that it is not a muzzle.

Due to the fact that this type of collar will cause dogs higher stress than any other kind, I generally don't recommend it. However, it is a good management tool.

BELIEVE IT OR NOT!

I had a darling student, a Maltese named Rocky, that barked at everyone on the bike path in Palm Beach. It was quite funny to see a well-groomed Rocky, at four pounds, terrorizing every large-sized dog on the path. His ever-active mother struggled day after day on her walks. We worked with Rocky every day for ten days. The very last day I said, "Mrs. Balboa, Rocky is much better, but he is not where we need him to be. I am going to try something I don't think I have ever tried on a Maltese, much less such a little one." I showed her a very small prong collar and how to use it on my wrist first. I then put it on her wrist so she could feel what Rocky would feel. "Let's do it!" she conceded, and Rocky became a different dog. He stopped even thinking about barking at everyone immediately. We gave him one small correction and after that he continued walking happy as the little man who owned the bike trail. We were both amazed. Mrs. Balboa calls me every now and then to say hello. She tells me Rocky misses me and that he is doing wonderfully on his walks.

The **prong collar**, I have been told, looks like a medieval torture device. The advantage of this collar is that it will do most of the work for you. The major downsides to the prong collar are (1) it can come undone leaving you without a dog on the end of the leash, and (2) you don't really finesse your handling skills or timing as well as you would with other collars. Nevertheless, I strongly recommend it for some dog and owner combinations. This collar works perfectly for certain dogs because it delivers just the right correction for that dog.

A relatively new product on the market is the **citronella collar**, which emits a squirt of citronella into the dog's face each time he barks. These collars also come with a remote that can be pressed from a distance, which will emit the scent. Some dogs will learn that if they step back as they bark, they will avoid the spray. This is not one of not my favorite tools, but if your dog has a barking problem and you want an inexpensive fast fix, then don't hesitate to use one.

Remember, however, this collar doesn't work on all dogs, and some dogs simply become conditioned not to bark when the collar is on them. Nothing beats good training. Since I have mentioned the citronella collar, I think I should also mention another collar, which like the citronella collar, also works on the operant conditioning concept.

The **electronic collar** is widely used in different formats: as an underground fence system, an anti-bark collar that can be found in your local pet shop, or a remote collar, which can be used to correct poor habits and teach obedience skills. There is probably no training tool that elicits such venomous opposition among trainers as the remote electronic collar.

There are a great number of advantages to this type of collar, which works on operant conditioning. You can gain off-leash control over your dog in no time at all. If you choose to utilize this tool, be sure to work with an experienced trainer when introducing your dog to the collar. Not all collars are the same. The old adage "you get what you pay for" really holds true for an electronic collar. Before

CASE IN POINT

Children kept tormenting an Australian Shepherd. The dog would chase and bark at them from "behind" an underground fence. As will any breed that is teased, the Aussie eventually bit someone. The breeder blamed the underground fence for the dog's aggression and insisted the owners purchase a regular fence. The breeder was mistaken. She failed to realize that it was not the fence. What happened was that the tormented dog finally got close enough to bite his tormentors. The actual teasing created the aggression. With a chain-link fence the dog will be tormented even more because now the children can come closer to the dog and poke the dog with sticks through the fence. This will antagonize the dog even more.

I worked with a Belgian Malinois. He was fittingly called Trouble. He would play in the yard in the afternoon. The fence was a tall wood stockade–style fence, which did not allow Trouble to see the other side. Each day children would come and knock on the wood and poke sticks through, antagonizing Trouble. One day a board fell off the post, and Trouble, finally seeing who was tormenting him, was able to get out and chased after them and bit one of the kids just as the Australian Shepherd had done. It is only a matter of time: a dog will escape and attack his tormenters, no matter whether he is behind a fence with no vision, a chain-link style, or an underground fence.

you get one, try one on your wrist. It feels like a tickle. If you have ever touched a bad switch, that is exactly what it feels like. It doesn't hurt, but it does startle you. Research collars before you purchase one and discuss their use with an experienced professional. When you use the collar correctly, you will see unbelievable results. I know of a quadriplegic who only had use of a couple of fingers who owned a very large Labrador Retriever. He couldn't even give his own dog a treat. His dog trainer suggested he use a remote electronic collar. Within an hour of the trainer working with the owner and the dog, the owner had complete control over the dog. Not only was the dog listening and paying attention, he happily wagged his tail the entire time.

Some with no experience will tell you that the electronic collar causes aggression. I know of several trainers who use it exclusively on aggressive dogs and are able to completely cure their behavior.

A **vibrating collar** works on the same premise as an electronic collar. However, instead of producing a shock or tickle, it vibrates, similar to a cell phone or beeper. This tool can be wonderful for deaf dogs. It can also be used on older dogs that have already been trained but due to old age don't hear as well as they used to.

A **five-foot leather leash** is the type of leash I recommend for training your dog. For years schools have recommended the six-foot leash, but for most women the six-foot is too long. You also want a leash that is no wider than ¾ inch. You will have difficulty finding this size leash, but you can order them online at HaggertyDog .com. Do not waste your money on a leash that is 1 inch wide. It is too wide for feminine hands. If you get a ½-inch-wide leash, it will be too thin, unless you have a toy-sized dog. If you prefer not to use leather, then get a hemp leash. I recommend hemp over cotton or nylon because it doesn't rub in your hand the way cotton and nylon do. It is also a stronger fabric so it will last longer for you.

A **twenty-foot cotton web leash** will help you with our distance work with your dog. Ideally you want to use a thirty-foot leash, but the twenty-foot is a good place to start so you can get used to the length. If the leash is shorter than twenty feet, it won't give us the foundation we need for off-leash work. Stick to one that is ¾ inch wide. Do not purchase a retractable type of leash, which can be tricky to use. For the sake of simplicity, we will not be using that type of leash. However, it is a good tool when used properly.

A **flat buckle collar** is imperative with or without training. We will use this collar for certain parts of the training so make sure you have one for your dog. I recommend a flat collar instead of a rolled collar. I have found that leather collars with a reflective strip are the safest and most practical. Of course, if you have a toy dog, a small nylon collar with rhinestones always looks nice. Hang your dog's rabies tag and owner information on a ring attached to the collar. Instead of an *S* hook, use a key ring to attach the tags. Make sure that you have a sturdy buckle and consistently check your dog's collar and tags to ensure they aren't in need of repair. This collar should be left on your dog at all times. Remember, a lost pet can't call home, but a collar with identification tags will enable someone to make the call for your pet.

Treats can be anything from small bite-sized pieces of cheese to cooked and sliced hot dogs. My personal favorite is freeze-dried liver. It comes in bite-sized pieces, dogs love it, and it isn't messy.

As far as treats are concerned, you will see that several commands have an approach using treats as the lure or reward. I have seen countless times dogs that were not weaned off of treats properly and the owners were married to their use forever. The average dog owner doesn't have the knowledge to read a dog and realize when to wean from the treats. Reading a dog and knowing how, and most importantly, when to wean from the treats are skills that require a lot of practice. Treats are great, especially for puppies under four months, but use them judiciously.

We won't be using all of the tools discussed in this chapter for every command, but we will want most of them available to us.

TREATS MAKE IT SWEETER

You do want to be careful when using treats. Many times dogs will be driven for the treat and though they are staring intently at you, it does not necessarily mean that they are listening to you; they may just be following the food and doing what they have to do to get it. When using treats, use them as a slot machine treats a gambler:

1. Don't let your dog get the treat every time.
2. Once she really starts responding, make sure that it is to you and not the treat.
3. Start giving treats to her less frequently.
4. Do not use at predictable intervals.
5. As soon as she starts responding, start weaning her off, almost immediately.

Walk This Way . . . and Give Her a Kiss

Work is either fun or drudgery. It depends on your attitude. I like fun.

—Colleen Barrett

TOOLS NEEDED FOR TEACHING THE HEEL COMMAND

training collar
five-foot leash
treats
twenty minutes

Eileen and her German Shepherd Dog, Star, started private lessons recently. As she was telling me her history with her nine-month-old dog, Eileen said she had attempted to train Star herself. One day they were walking, and Star saw something in the woods. They both ended up on the ground, and Eileen said to herself, "This is not working. I think that it is time for some help."

If you have found yourself in a similar situation, you are not alone. Many dog owners have called me over the years with sprained wrists, broken fingers, and twisted ankles. They had all attempted to walk their untrained dogs, and they have all found themselves in need of some help.

You may have children, perhaps a career, and possibly a significant other. You want your dog to walk loosely on your left side and not to pull when she sees other dogs.

We are going to take the heel command from several different approaches. If one doesn't work for you and your Star, try another approach. If you don't see results after the first practice session,

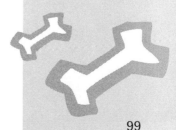

then try another approach. The proper heel position is when your dog walks next to you on your left side. Your left leg should be in line with her shoulder.

Prepare for Success

Treat 'em like dogs, and you'll have dogs' works and dogs' actions. Treat 'em like men, and you'll have men's works.

—Harriet Beecher Stowe

Just as athletes prepare mentally and physically for success, you too are going to prepare so that both you and your dog succeed.

Deep-Breathing Exercises

Before we get started, I want you to go to a quiet area and then do as follows:

1. Sit down and close your eyes.
2. Take deep breaths. Inhale for a count of four and exhale for a count of four, very slowly and deeply.
3. Continue to inhale and fill your lungs and exhale all of the air out of your lungs until you are feeling relaxed.

Positive Visualization

Each day before training I want you to practice visualization exercises. Keep your eyes closed and start thinking about your wonderfully sweet girl. Picture yourself walking down the street with her at your left-hand side. She keeps looking up at you so adoringly with those big, dark brown, innocent eyes. You pass several children and dogs. She keeps walking next to you without pulling. She doesn't even chase the squirrel that just ran in front of you. You stop to chat with your neighbor while she sits down waiting for you. She doesn't move until you start heading home. She just seems to be attached to you. Open your eyes. Isn't that a nice thought?

Positive Affirmation

Once you have done your visualization exercises, look in the mirror and say, "I have a great dog. She and I are going to have fun today. We are going to learn a lot from one another. I am not going to worry about anything else because I am going to give Star fifteen minutes of quality time training her. Everything is going to get done. I am not going to think about all of my other responsibilities." Such positive affirmation may seem a little silly, especially for a book on dog training, but we women worry and can very often take on more than we should. We know how to multitask much better than men; therefore, it is not uncommon that we cook dinner, help with homework, and close a deal via the cell phone, while attempting to train the dog. If we are not doing all of these things at one time, our minds are on those other tasks. So for once, try to forget everything. Put it all aside and give fifteen minutes to train Star. Don't worry: you are a woman, and you will get it all done.

Now this is where it gets weird. We are going to first train you before we train your dog. Let me explain: When my dad was writing *Zen and the Art of Dog Training*, he gave me the draft and asked me to experiment. He wanted me to teach the footwork, the hand signals, and the body movements of all the commands to the people before they brought their dogs to class. We call these "exercises" *katas*. We started this new method immediately, and the difference was amazing! The dogs were calmer in class, the owners were having fun, our graduation rate accelerated, and the dropout rate dimin-

WOMEN CAN DO IT ALL!

I remember I was flying to a dog show in Germany. As I was preparing for my trip, my dad laughed and said, "Babette, it is funny that you can run two businesses, raise a baby, write two books, and take care of yourself when it is just you and Gordon. However, when you leave town, you need to hire help and fly people in to cover everything and those people still can't handle it as well as you alone." I answered, "I am a woman. We can do it all."

ished drastically. We realized that once the owners were confident in what they needed to do, it was easier for them and they held a less tension-filled leash, which goes right down the line to the dog. The dogs learned more quickly as well.

Another interesting note is that although we were spending one week less with the dogs, we actually had time to teach additional commands. We were accomplishing more in less time.

Katas

Now before we take your dog outside, let's train you first. We are going to start with the elephant's trunk kata to help you learn how to use the leash effectively:

1. Stand up straight and relaxed with your feet either together or shoulder-width apart.
2. Keep your arms down and relaxed.
3. Swing your right arm out to the side, similar to the pendulum of a grandfather's clock.
4. Bring your right arm back to your side.
5. Start moving your right arm out and in.
6. While moving your right arm out and in, start walking around while saying, "Heel." Keep doing this kata for the next one minute. Stop and give yourself lots of praise. Now do it again. Do it for another minute, walking in a circle saying, "Heel, heel, heel." Make sure you keep moving your arm out and in, while you keep your left arm straight down and relaxed at your side. What you are administering is called a "correction." Timed properly, it is an effective and fair way to stop your dog from doing the wrong thing, in this case, pulling on the leash.

Recently the *Palm Beach Post* published a full-page story about me, and the headline read, "Dog Trainer Discovers Her Work Applies to Training Toddlers Too." Raising my child and training my dogs had made me realize that my parents taught me the difference between right and wrong because they stopped me from doing the wrong thing and encouraged the right thing.

If your dog wasn't doing anything wrong, you wouldn't have needed this book, now would you? Remember we need to set your

Keep your arms straight down and relaxed. Photo by www.mortonimages.com.

Swing your right arm out to your side. Photo by www.mortonimages.com.

Bring your right arm back to your side. Keep it straight down and relaxed. Photo by Gordon Brennan.

Quickly move your right arm out and in. Keep your arms and shoulders relaxed, and don't forget to breathe. Photos by Gordon Brennan.

dog up to succeed by showing her the right way and stopping the bad behaviors.

Which Collar for My Dog?

I mentioned several collars in the last chapter. Every dog and owner needs a different collar. What will work for you and your dog, will not work for your neighbor's dog. I am going to make general recommendations based on the "type" of dog you have.

With the exception of the flat buckle collar, these are not collars to keep on your dog permanently. They should only be worn during training sessions and under supervision.

We will address the use of a prong collar or a Halti later. For right now I would like you to start with one of the following collars. Certain collars are better suited to certain dogs.

Flat Buckle Collar

This is the only collar to keep on your dog permanently. You will want to put her nametag and rabies tag on the ring of the collar. I recommend using a ring from a key chain, as opposed to the *S* hook that usually comes with a dog nametag. The key chain ring will stay on longer, has less chance of getting caught on something, and is usually made from a longer lasting metal. For training, this collar works well for young puppies under five or six month of age and small breeds, such as a Maltese or a Cavalier King Charles Spaniel.

Training Choker Chain

The training choker chain is suitable for a large breed puppy older than six months—for example, Labrador Retrievers, German Shepherds, and Soft-Coated Wheaten Terriers. Follow the steps in Chapter 4 for placing the choker chain collar on your dog properly.

Fitted Collar

A fitted collar is suitable for any large, full-grown dog. To ensure a proper fit, follow the directions given in Chapter 4.

Martingale Collar

The Martingale collar is good for Sighthounds—a subgroup of the Hound group that includes Afghan Hounds, Borzois, Greyhounds, Ibizan Hounds, Irish Wolfhounds, Pharaoh Hounds, Salukis, Scottish Deerhounds, and Whippets—no matter their age. See Chapter 4 for directions on properly putting this collar on your dog.

Before you put any collar on your dog, I would like for you to practice putting it on the wrist of a friend first. Have your friend hold out his or her right wrist as you place the collar on it as though you were facing your dog.

Holding the Leash

Just as there is a proper way to put a collar on your dog, there is a proper way to hold a leash. Follow these directions:

1. Place your right thumb through the loop.
2. Lay the loop in the palm of your right hand.
3. Keeping your thumb through the loop, slide your right hand halfway down the leash and lay it over your right index finger.

4. Lay the rest in your right palm.
5. Wrap your right hand around the leash, keeping it looped around your thumb and index finger.
6. Leave the leash loose with slack. Do not attempt to pick up the slack in your left hand.

Remember the elephant's trunk kata? I want you to practice this kata on a friend's arm. Put the collar on her wrist, take the leash, and practice snapping the leash. If your friend feels anything, then you are holding your arm out to the side and not returning it quickly

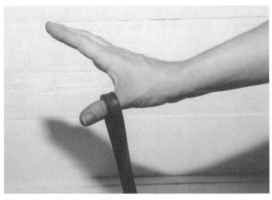

Right thumb through the loop. Photo by www.mortonimages.com.

Lay the loop in the palm of your right hand. Photo by www.mortonimages.com.

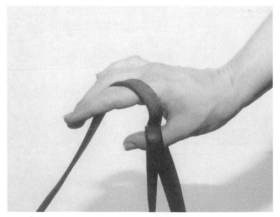

Keeping your thumb in the loop, slide your right hand halfway down the leash and place that over your right index finger. Photo by www.mortonimages.com.

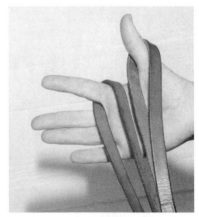

Lay the rest comfortably in your right hand. Photo by www.mortonimages.com.

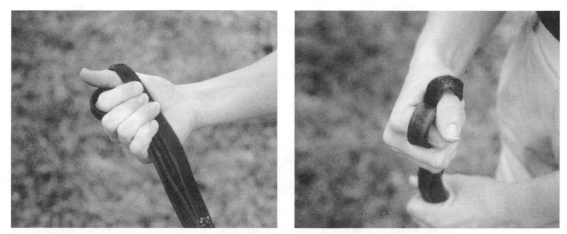

Wrap your right hand around the leash. It is still looped around your thumb and index finger.
Photos by Gordon Brennan.

This leash has slack. You need to have slack. This is imperative. Photo by Gordon Brennan.

This leash has no slack. This is not correct.
Photo by www.mortonimages.com.

There is slack, and my arm is straight down and relaxed. Photo by www.mortonimages.com.

My arm is out to the side, swinging like an elephant's trunk. Photo by www.mortonimages.com.

I bring the arm back in quickly. Gordon felt nothing. Photos by www.mortonimages.com.

Nice, quick, and easy. A student practices on my arm. Photo by Susan King.

Another student makes certain that she returns her arm quickly, keeping slack in the leash. Again, I feel nothing. Photo by Susan King.

enough. It should be a quick movement. You have it right when your friend tells you that she has felt nothing. You will notice in the photos that follow that all arms are returning back to the side in the relaxed position and that there is slack in the leash. Do this over and over again, until you hear a quick click, then click and release. It is imperative that you are good at this before practicing on your dog. Practice between six and eight snaps and you will have it down pat.

Teaching your dog to walk on your left side in the heel position is the most work physically for you. This phase of the training will give you the foundation in your leash handling skills. In the next couple of days you will see a big difference in your dog. She will be calmer and happier. We are going to take several approaches to working with your dog on the leash, but for each approach keep the following in mind:

- Encouragement is essential.
- We need to praise often and with enthusiasm.
- Your dog may need to be stopped from doing wrong. Not only do we need to teach Star what is right but also what is wrong. We don't want to nag her endlessly. It is too draining for you and for her. We want to stop bad behavior and move on. All dogs need discipline.

Approach #1

Let's put the collar and leash on your dog and take her outside. Start with the leash in your right hand and come halfway down on the leash. Place your dog on your left side and practice the following steps:

1. Start with your left foot first.
2. Say, "Heel."
3. Pat your left leg and start walking.
4. Talk to her as you walk. Tell her what a good girl she is.
5. If she gets ahead of you, turn to your right, and walk in the opposite direction. This is called the about-turn.

6. If she pulls off to the side, give a quick tug.

7. Once she moves in closer, stop and give her praise.

8. Start again.

9. Take three steps, stop, and praise her again.

10. If she continues to pull and you have given her a quick tug to

I start heeling Java with my left foot. She is happy as I talk to her and encourage her along.

Photo by Gordon Brennan.

Trainer Jill Hendelman turns away from Brutus as he gets ahead of her. She walks in the opposite direction. This is the about-turn. Photo by Babette Haggerty-Brennan.

Soupie is heeling too far to the left.

Photo by Gordon Brennan.

This leash is too tight to fairly correct Java for being too far away. Make sure that it is loose and has slack.

Photo by Gordon Brennan.

We praise Java throughout her practice session. Photo by Gordon Brennan.

correct her but she is not responding, you are not doing it effectively. Tug while the leash is loose, not when it is tight.

11. Make sure that as she walks right next to you, you stroke her ear or the top of her head. She will associate walking next to you with lots of love and affection.

12. Constantly practice this over and over. Don't forget to stop and praise a lot.

Q&A

She keeps pulling back, fighting the leash. What's wrong?

She may not be leash broken. While she is wearing her leash, crouch down and tap your left ankle, gently calling her to you. Once she takes a step, stop, and give her lots of praise. Keep doing that. You can also help her get leash broken by letting her drag the leash around the house, under supervision.

My little dog won't walk away from the house, only toward it. What can I do?

Toy dogs are the most difficult to leash break and to teach to heel. With her leash on, take her away from the house and start walking in the direction of the house, while you say, "Heel." She will run ahead of you, but as soon as she does, stop and give her lots of praise.

My dog hooks the end of the leash with her paw. How do I gain control?

You quite possibly have a mixed breed. They seem to be the ones that are smart enough to know that if they can control the leash then you cannot. Once your dog hooks the leash, look at her, loosen the leash, and in an encouraging tone say, "Heel, good girl!" and start taking small, rapid steps. Once she starts walking toward you, take two more steps, stop, and give her lots of praise.

If I start walking and she starts wrapping herself behind me on the wrong side, what should I do?

Keep walking, and while you do that, take your left hand and pull the leash around. Do not stop; otherwise, she will learn how to take control of the situation. Remember not to look at her on the right side. Looking at her is a form of praise, and if you praise her while she is on the wrong side, it will take longer to teach her to walk on the correct side.

I feel very uncomfortable not holding the leash in my left hand. I feel like I have no control. Is there a solution?

Most people feel this way at first, but you will get used to it. You have a better range of motion when the leash is in your right hand. If you try snapping the leash with your left hand (or both hands), your body will get in the way. Moreover, if you keep the leash in your left hand (or both hands), you are more apt to hold the leash tightly and thereby restrain your dog. The more you restrain, the more she will pull away from you. The more slack you have, the more control you have. A truly trained dog can walk down the street being held by a piece of string.

My Italian Greyhound is so timid and shy. She doesn't want to walk that far with me. Am I doing something wrong?

No. This is perfectly normal. Keep her on the left side and start walking. Look over your shoulder and say, "Heel, good girl." If she takes half a step, say, "Good girl. You are so good."

I have a very exuberant Lab. She keeps jumping up on me and grabbing the leash. Will she ever stop?

Tell her no. Give the leash a quick pop and start walking again. Each time she jumps up, correct her and tell her no. By the third time, she will never do it again.

My dog just drops and won't walk. Is there any hope?

Yes, of course there is. Don't stop walking. Just keep encouraging her. Use a happy tone and take little baby steps rapidly away from her. Give a slight tug on the leash and then tell her to heel.

What do I do when I just want to take her for a bathroom walk?

You can use her bathroom walk to practice heeling. Heel her to the same spot each day for her bathroom walks. Step back while giving her extra leash to sniff around and give her the command to "go potty." At this point she needn't be in the heel position. Once she has relieved herself, bring her back into the heel position and start heeling her back to the house.

It will take me forever to get around the block. Why can't I just let her have her nice walks?

It is important that we are consistent in the training. You don't want her to learn that sometimes she has to heel and sometimes she doesn't. It is important during the training process that we maintain the proper heel position at all times. Once we have her trained, her walks can be a shorter distance. The stricter you are now, the better result you will have and the happier you both will be in the end.

Approach #2

Put a couple of your dog's favorite cookies in your left hand and show them to your dog. Keep the leash in your right hand and hold out a cookie in your left. Start walking, saying, "Heel," to have her follow the treat. Once she takes a few steps, stop, and give her the cookie and lots of praise. This is not something you want to do for very long. As soon as she starts responding to the cookies, start weaning her off them.

Q&A

My dog keeps jumping up trying to grab the cookie. What's a girl to do?

Don't let her do that. If she does, stop, give the leash a quick snap, tell her no, and move on and start again.

My dog seems so focused on the cookie. I don't feel like she is paying attention to me. Help!

She probably isn't. She is driven by the food and that is her sole motivator. Stop using the cookies.

Why doesn't my dog like any of the treats that I give her?

Some dogs are just not motivated by food. Try a different lure such as a toy.

Management Approach

Perhaps you are at your wit's end. You just can't take Star for a walk without being pulled. You are mentally drained and you find yourself having to walk her at odd hours so that she doesn't see other dogs. Get her to training class immediately! Until you do, buy a head halter and start using it. It won't teach her to walk next to you naturally without the leash, but it will manage her pulling behavior to make life easier for you until you solve the problem.

To introduce her to the head halter, you want to confirm that you have the right size for her. Check the packaging. Refer to Chapter 4 for directions on how to put this type of collar on your dog properly.

You may find that your dog's first reaction is to paw at the head halter to pull it off her muzzle, or she may jerk herself around. Stand calmly. Don't pull at her leash or attempt to take the collar off. If you give her a minute, she will eventually stop fighting. When you take her outside and start walking her, she may fight it more. If she does, just stop and wait for her to relax. Give her a treat or two or just be loving. She most likely won't take the treat, but loving strokes will help soothe her. To be honest, this can be very stressful for your dog, and some dogs take longer than others to get used to the head halter. That is one reason why this collar is not my favorite tool, but we need to do what will work best for you.

Q&A

My dog keeps fighting the head halter. Is this OK?

Some dogs take a very long time to get used to it. If she continues to paw at it and bucks while wearing it, stop walking and just wait for her to relax. Some dogs, such as Rottweilers, will really continue to resent the halter. Realize that the halter is something that is pulling her around by her muzzle. She has no choice where to walk. It is similar to someone pulling you around by a nose ring—like a bull. When your dog is wearing a choker chain or fitted collar, she makes a decision as to where to walk and learns that life is best right next to you. With the halter she is forced to walk next to you, without choice on her part.

People keep asking me if this is a muzzle. I get so angry. How should I respond?

Don't. Everyone is an expert, and everyone has an opinion. Just tell them no and ignore them.

If you are not crazy about this halter thing, why are you recommending it?

It is a good management tool and if it is going to get you through until you can start good formal training, then I will recommend just about anything. This is also a good management tool for people who have a dog much larger than they or for people who have severe arthritis and have trouble with their hands and controlling their dog.

Challenges Women Face with Teaching the Heel Command

If you are larger on top, you may have trouble with your range of motion when correcting your dog. To compensate for this, you want small, snappy movements. You can bend your knees a little bit and crouch down about three inches to give a proper snap on the lead.

If you are petite, your dog may very well outweigh you. If this is the case, keep your leash a little shorter so that there is less slack, and use a high choker chain or a fitted collar on your dog.

HOMEWORK
- Practice heeling for about fifteen minutes each day.
- Do this for the next three days.
- Remember that you can practice heeling even when you just want to take your dog out for a bathroom walk.

DAILY PRACTICE CHECKLIST
- Did I practice my deep breathing exercise?
- Did I do my positive visualization?
- Did I practice my positive affirmation?
- Did I continually praise my dog, telling her that she is a great dog?
- Is my arm straight down and relaxed?
- Are my shoulders relaxed?
- Am I moving my arm out and returning quickly?
- Am I talking to my dog the whole time in a happy voice?

Sit on It

Dogs lives are too short. Their only fault, really.

—Agnes Sligh Turnbull

TOOLS NEEDED FOR TEACHING THE AUTOMATIC-SIT

training collar
five-foot leash
calm voice
ten minutes

I remember the after-school special "It Must Be Love, Because I Feel So Dumb," which aired on ABC in 1975. My Golden Retriever, Muffin, played the part of child actor Alfred Lutter's only friend. The end was traumatic, not because he was rejected by the girl he liked but because he stopped at a curb to tie his shoe. He didn't put Muffin in an automatic-sit, she saw something across the street, she ran, and got hit by a car and killed. Yes, this was television, but I still remember sobbing and clinging on to Muffin while I watched her die on national television. Now granted it wasn't in the script, but in real life if he had put her in an automatic-sit while he tied his shoe, she would have stayed in the sit position and not been killed. This fictional tale gives you the real-world reason for this command.

This is almost not a command and more of a routine habit. What automatic-sit means is that when you stop walking, your Muffin will sit next to you without you telling her to sit. The practical application for this is that any time you stop walking, you want Muffin to sit. It will make your life easier. For example, you stop to talk to the neighbor. The automatic-sit will decrease the chances of your Muffin pulling to jump on the neighbor's dog or pulling you into the street. It will keep her more focused on you.

Based on your body type and the type of dog you have, the techniques of teaching this command will vary. A big difference between women and men is that men tend to have more upper body strength. Men are also (on average) taller than we are, so they have a higher center point making this command easier for them than for women. Some of us women carry a lot more weight on top than others, which also affects how we teach this command. The height and weight of your dog will also affect the way this is taught.

Prepare for Success

If you want success, you've got to prepare for it both physically and mentally. This applies to success in training your dog too.

Breathing Exercises

Put away your cell phone and go to a quiet place. Practice the deep-breathing exercises as discussed in Chapter 5.

Positive Visualization

Picture yourself walking down the street. You are going to come to a very busy intersection, which you must cross. You will see a dog across the street, but once you come to the curb, Muffin is going to stop, although the other dog is barking at her to play. Muffin is going to stay next to you waiting at the curb until you both start walking again. Once you cross the street, you are going to encounter your neighbor with her new puppy. This time as soon as you stop, Muffin will also sit, although the puppy is beckoning to her to play.

Positive Affirmation

Once you have done your visualization exercises, look in the mirror and say, "This will be easy. My dog learns these things very easily. I will have her sitting automatically for me by the end of the session."

Katas

I am going to have you go through the motions without Muffin, so do not take her outside yet. So that you understand exactly what is going to happen to Muffin, I would like for you to stand up. Tilt your head back, lifting up your chin. You will notice that as you lift up your chin and tilt your head back, your pelvis tucks underneath. Your weight shifts, which is also going to happen with Muffin, with one exception. When her weight shifts, she automatically goes into a sit position.

There are two parts to this exercise. This first part gets you ready to convey the body language to Muffin to stop. She is going to sense you slowing down. The second part teaches her to sit, once you stop.

PART ONE

1. Walk alone.
2. Slow down your pace.
3. Slowly lift up your left arm as though you were doing a bicep curl.
4. Stop.

Make sure you keep your elbow in and your left hand is closed.

PART TWO

1. Stand with your arms at your side.
2. Bend your arms in front of you.
3. Place your right palm up to the sky.
4. Place your left palm down to the ground.
5. Simultaneously, move your arms in opposite directions. Do that three times.
6. Now you are going to do it again, except you are going to move in an arc.
7. Start with your right hand at 3:00 and your left at 9:00. As you move them simultaneously, you are going to end up with your right hand at 1:00 and your left at 7:00.

Place your arms in front with the right palm facing up and the left palm facing down. Photo by www.mortonimages.com.

Repeat this motion three times. Photo by www.mortonimages.com.

8. Visualize a teeter-totter. When you stand alongside a teeter-totter and reverse which side is up, the action is the same as your arms. You are shifting the weight.

As a woman there are some other things that you need to keep in mind. You may not have strong biceps. To compensate make sure that when you start pulling up on the leash you are holding the leash using a strong grip. Face your palm down and make sure that your wrist is straight and that when you grab the leash you take the leash from the left side. In other words, make sure you don't place your hand between your body and the leash and twist your wrist out to grab the leash. This is very important. If you do this incorrectly you put unnecessary strain on your wrist and you will have no strength when you lift.

Approach #1

Before we go outside, let us get our leash, collar, treat or toy, and most importantly, Muffin.

The automatic-sit is quite simple. It is a ten-step process. Once you do this a half dozen times, Muffin will be sitting for you in no time.

1. Start heeling.
2. Slow down your pace.
3. Put your left hand on the leash and start picking up the slack, like the bicep curl that you practiced. Make sure you have a firm grip and a straight wrist.
4. Once you do this, stop.

I slow down as I pick up the leash. Photo by Gordon Brennan.

I have a firm grip and a straight wrist. Photo by Gordon Brennan.

I don't grab the leash like this. This puts a strain on your wrist and is not a firm grip. Photo by Gordon Brennan.

We lift Lili's muzzle, shifting her weight. We do not push down on her rear. Photo by www.mortonimages.com.

We mold Baxter into position by shifting his weight. Photo by www.mortonimages.com.

We say, "Sit," very softly. Photo by www.mortonimages.com.

We give Baxter lots of praise. This is immediate because our hands are already on him, giving him love and encouragement. Photo by www.mortonimages.com.

5. Turn to your left facing your dog.
6. Take your right hand and place it under your dog's muzzle, lifting it in an arc.
7. While you lift up your dog's muzzle, touch her rear end with your left hand, and place it into the downward arc that we practiced. Do *not* push down on her rear. You want to cradle it.
8. While you do this, say, "Sit," softly.
9. Once your dog sits, your hands are already on her. Give her lots of love and praise. You can release her with a treat or a toy.
10. Repeat several times.

You will notice that after doing this a few times, your dog will start sitting for you without you prompting her as much. Once she starts improving in that aspect, usually after the third time, she will start to respond when you start picking up the leash in your left hand. Keep in mind that you are not lifting her off the ground. You are picking up the slack and decreasing the amount that is already there.

Q&A

It seems that as I start to slow down, she keeps going, so should I pull her back?

Instead of pulling her back, give the leash a quick pop with your right hand and pull up with the left and make her sit.

As I lift up on her muzzle, she starts to stand on her hindquarters and squirm. What am I doing wrong?

You are probably lifting her head, not tilting her muzzle. There is a difference. You want to tilt her muzzle. Lift your own chin again so that you can refresh your memory of how you want to change her center of gravity.

I put my hand on her muzzle and as soon as I try to place her into the sit, she starts to freeze. How do I make this work?

Just relax, don't keep lifting. Just hold your dog and speak to her in a soft voice. As you do this, caress her back toward her tail very lightly and gently.

As soon as she sits, she gets back up again. Help!

Don't worry about that yet. We are going to work on the stay next.

Baxter sits automatically when I simply lift the leash up. Photo by www.mortonimages.com.

Whenever you stop to talk to a neighbor, always place your dog in an automatic-sit. Even a pregnant woman can do it with three dogs—multitasking at its finest! Photo by www.mortonimages.com.

Approach #2

This approach is most suitable for toy dogs and smaller dogs. You will do the same as you do for Approach #1 except you don't need to do the "bicep curl"; just gently lift the leash with your fingers and she will sit.

Now the trouble with small dogs is that it requires a lot of bending to get them to sit. Practice getting your dog to sit on a countertop or the top of the washing machine first. This way she is used to sitting, and it will be that much easier when you take her outside.

Approach #3

You can use this approach if you are a very tiny person and you have a very large breed of dog, such as a Mastiff. Do the same as you would in Approach #1, but don't touch your dog's rear end. Keep your strength in your arm and your balance in both feet. Sometimes you may lean over and then you don't have enough strength. You can also slightly bend your knees while leaning over her. That will give you more balance.

1. Lift up the leash with your left hand.
2. Lift up your dog's muzzle with your right hand.
3. Hold until she sits.
4. Give lots of praise.

Approach #4

If you would prefer to use the food approach, keep your treats hidden at first.

1. Start heeling.
2. Slow down your pace.
3. Take a treat out of your right-hand pocket.
4. Lift up the leash with your left hand.
5. Bring your right hand in front of your dog's face holding the treat.
6. Stop walking.
7. Place the treat in front of her nose.
8. Lift the treat in an arc, toward her eyes so that she lifts her muzzle.
9. As soon as she sits, give her the treat.

Remember that you should stop using treats as soon as your dog starts responding to them. The best way to do that is decrease the frequency: every other time, every fourth time, etc. However, if she quits sitting entirely the first time you stop the treats, do *not* revert back to them. There are no options. You have told her to sit. Place her into the sit by lifting her muzzle and shifting her weight. This is called molding behavior.

Q&A
When I give her the treat, she starts jumping up. How do I get her to stop?

You are not holding onto the leash properly with the left hand. You are giving her too much leeway. Correct her with a quick snap and once she sits, give her the treat.

She bites my fingers when she takes the treat. Is there a trick?

Hold the treat in your fist. Let her smell the treat in your closed fist. Once she stops using her teeth, then give her the treat.

HOMEWORK

- Practice the heel command (see Chapter 5).
- When you first take Muffin outside, begin by taking one step forward and place her into a sit.
- Take another step forward and place her into a sit.
- Take a third step forward and place her into a sit.
- After the third time, stop molding her into the sit. You will find that the more you practice, the more quickly you can stop physically prompting her. She will start going into a sit on her own, and as soon as her tushy hits the ground, give her lots of praise.
- Practice each day for about fifteen minutes.
- After four days, she will be sitting for you without any prompts.
- At that time, stop telling her to sit so that she learns to sit when you stop walking.

DAILY PRACTICE CHECKLIST

- Did I practice my breathing exercises?
- Did I do my positive visualization?
- Did I practice my positive affirmation?
- Am I relaxed?
- Am I using a calm, quiet tone?
- Do I slow down before I place her into a sit?
- Am I placing her into a sit or pushing into a sit? (Make sure you are molding her into a sit, not pushing.)
- Do I praise my dog immediately?

Stayin' Alive

My little dog: A heartbeat at my feet.

—*Edith Wharton*

TOOLS NEEDED FOR TEACHING THE SIT-STAY COMMAND

training collar
five-foot leash
twenty-foot leash
treats
fifteen minutes

You may think that the title of this chapter is odd, but the stay command can actually save your dog's life. The McCarthys hired me for private lessons for their Labrador Retriever puppy. They told me their last dog was hit by a car and killed because she ran out the front door one day when the door was opened for visitors. "If we took Ginger to class and taught her to stay at the front door, she would be alive today. We don't want to ever have to see that again."

It is very important that dogs know the sit-stay. Initially, the command calms them down. They learn not to run out the front door, to sit calmly when they meet someone, to stay still when you sit in the waiting room at the veterinary clinic. The list is endless. It is difficult to qualify and state that any command is more useful than another, but this command is one that can be used a dozen times a day.

We are going to teach your Ginger to sit-stay for three minutes minimum with distractions. I know that you are sitting there with great doubt. You believe your dog could never sit still for that long. I am going to show you how, and in less than one week, she will be doing that for you.

EVEN I WAS IMPRESSED!

Many years ago, I had the opportunity to work with a really neat woman named Gale. She owned the Kentucky Derby winner, Strike the Gold, and lived in a prestigious polo community. She had Amadeus, a gorgeous black Standard Poodle, one of my favorite breeds. As with all my students I trained Amadeus to never go through any door unless invited to do so. He was trained to sit and stay on the cue of any open door. One day Gale's son went out through the garage to a friend's house leaving the garage door and house door open. About a half hour after the boy left, the secretary walked passed the back hall and saw Amadeus in a sit-stay. The family was thrilled. We all knew her son had not told him to sit and stay when he was leaving but that the dog knew to stay due to his training. Amadeus saw the open door and decided to stay until he was released.

Prepare for Success

Always be mindful that if you want success, you need to prepare for it.

Breathing Exercises

Go to a quiet place and practice the deep-breathing exercises discussed in Chapter 5.

Positive Visualization

For today's visualization exercise picture yourself putting Ginger in the car and then driving to Starbuck's. Once you get out of the car, before you open the door on Ginger's side, you are going to give her a hand signal for stay. You will open the car door. She sits there until you tell her to get out of the car. You will then heel her to a bench in front. You are going to tell her to sit and stay and tie her leash to the permanently affixed chair. You will go inside the front door and order your Doppio Macchiato with a shot of soy milk. You need the energy, right? The entire time you are inside, everyone is coming over to pet your beautiful dog. They are going to fuss all over her. You are going to proudly watch through the window and see her waiting attentively for you. Although she will be enjoying all of the attention, she is not going to move. After all, you did tell her to sit and stay. When you go outside to praise her, everyone is going to compliment you on your well-behaved dog. They will ask where she was trained. You will proudly say, "We girls did it together, by ourselves."

Katas

Before actually doing the following exercise, I want you to do some more deep breathing exercises. This is a good habit to establish. Breathe in for a count of four and breathe out for a count of four. And now you are ready for the staying alive two-step kata. As with the other commands we have learned, we need to figure out what we are going to do first without our dog.

1. Stand tall and comfortably.
2. Arms should hang down at your sides.
3. Place your left hand out to the side with the palm facing behind you. That is your hand signal for stay.
4. Pivot on the left foot, stepping over with the right foot.
5. Return.

Left hand to the side. Palm facing back. Photo by www.mortonimages.com.

Keeping hand in position, step over with right foot while pivoting on the left. Photo by www.mortonimages.com.

Now you are facing your invisible dog. Photo by www.mortonimages.com.

Everyone can do the staying alive two-step. Photo by Babette Haggerty-Brennan.

6. Repeat, but this time when you place your hand with your palm facing behind you say, "Stay."
7. Practice this three to four times.

Approach #1

Bring Ginger outside; give her a moment to relieve herself. Before we teach her this command, we want to work off some of that pent-up energy. Begin by heeling her for about five to ten minutes. Throw some automatic-sits into the routine. Great job! Now that we have prepared her and ourselves for a positive learning experience, we are ready to start teaching your dog the sit-stay:

1. Begin by heeling Ginger and ending with an automatic-sit, just as we did to warm up.
2. Keep the leash in your right hand. This time keep it very short, virtually without slack.
3. Place your left hand out to the side with the palm facing your dog.
4. She should still be sitting. Now say, "Stay."

5. Put your left hand on her left cheek.

6. Step in front of her with your right foot. Make sure that you pivot on the left foot. Stay very close to her.

7. Very slowly move around her. Keep the leash very short with your hand remaining on her left cheek. As you move around, calmly tell her to stay. You want to repeat this over and over again. You can also stop, cradle her head, and give her lots of calm, soft praise.

8. Return to her right side.

9. Give lots of love and praise.

I am showing Baxter my left hand signal. Photo by www.mortonimages.com.

I show him the hand signal while facing him and say, "Stay." I keep the leash taut. Photo by www.mortonimages.com.

I keep my left hand on his cheek so I can praise him for staying while I move around and behind him. Photo by www.mortonimages.com.

I return to his side giving him lots of praise. Photo by www.mortonimages.com.

What we need to do next is to start lengthening the amount of time your dog stays. You want to repeat the steps above five to seven times, each time praising her and moving around slowly. You can even circle two or three times before you praise her. As long as you keep your hand on her cheek, stay close, and keep the leash short, she probably won't even try getting up.

If your dog should get up, you can give a quick snap of the leash, which you will have in your right hand—remember the elephant's trunk kata. You will be able to correct quickly with ease. Incidentally, it is anatomically impossible for her to get up without first lowering her head, just like in order for you to get up from a chair you need to lean forward first. That is your clue that she is going to get up. Another clue is if you see her shifting her weight. Keep the leash somewhat elevated and taut so that if she does start lowering her head or shifting her weight, you can step in and tell her no. Allow her to relax and shift her weight back again. Once you return to her side, give her lots of praise.

When you want to break her stay, choose some sort of release phrase such as "good girl" or "take a break." Some people use "OK,"

FUNNY STORY

Ilse is from Finland. She is a stunning girl with ocean blue eyes and long, blonde hair that no Hollywood hair guru could ever create. She would get out of her little black sports car and heads would turn to see this fair-haired girl get out of the car with her gorgeous Standard American Eskimo, which is larger than the popular Miniature American Eskimo. Karhu was appropriately named. His name means "Bear" in Finnish. Ilse had only been in the United States for a couple of years and was still learning English. One day Karhu just would not sit still in class. Knowing that Karhu knew what to do and assessing that there was no other reason for his not wanting to sit still, she asked me, "Why won't he sit still?" I replied, "Oh, he has ants in his pants." Poor Ilse screamed, "Oh, my gosh!" as she started rummaging through Karhu's thick white coat. I tried not to laugh while I stopped her. "Oh, Ilse, what I said is just an idiom. He does not really have ants in his pants." She felt much better. Her American husband had a good laugh with her about it.

but some dogs will respond to it even if you are just using it in conversation.

We want to set Ginger up for complete success so we are going to make sure that she doesn't get up from the stay. We must give her a quick break and begin again. We are going to start from the beginning and then expand on that to begin working on distance. Let us review:

1. Place Ginger in an automatic-sit.
2. Keep the leash in your right hand. Keep it very short, virtually without slack.
3. Place your left hand out to the side with the palm facing Ginger.
4. Say, "Stay."
5. Step in front of her face.
6. Stand right in front of her.

This is the difference:

7. Slowly back up. As you back up, keep the leash taut. This is very important.

This is correct—not too much slack—stopping Punky from getting up. Photo by Babette Haggerty-Brennan.

There is too much slack. If Lexi starts to get up, Gordon will be unable to correct her. Photo by Babette Haggerty-Brennan.

Make sure you gather the leash as you move in. Photo by www.mortonimages.com.

8. While backing up continue to say, "Stay," and show her the hand signal. Keep your right hand through the loop, and holding the extra leash with your left hand, you are ready to stop her from getting up.

9. Move in toward her, making sure to gather the leash. You don't want any excess leash hanging down.

10. Put your left hand on her left cheek.

11. Very slowly move around her. Keep the leash very short with your hand remaining on her left cheek. As you move around, calmly tell her to stay.

12. Return to her right side.

13. Give lots of love and praise.

As you start to work on distance, your dog is bound to get up; however, we don't want her to have to be corrected for getting up. We want to convince her to not think about getting up. It is all in the timing. Remember that it is anatomically impossible for her to get up without lowering her head first. When she starts to lower her head, tell her no. If she starts lying down instead of sitting, don't worry about it. I will accept that. She is less likely to get up from a down. Unless you are going to compete in obedience, if she lies down, allow it.

Q&A

She keeps getting up. What do I do?

Remember to watch her head. Go back to the basic steps in Approach #1. Don't worry about the distance yet. Take care of the length of time first. Then introduce the extended distance.

Approach #2

If you are petite or have an exceptionally large dog such as a Great Dane, you want to do the same thing as in Approach #1, but as you

Lili is a big girl, so I softly cradle her head while I tell her to stay. I'm setting her up for success. Photo by www.mortonimages.com.

stand in front of your dog, you want to gently cradle your dog's head in each hand. In other words, you will have your right hand on her left cheek and your left hand on her right cheek.

1. Look lovingly into her eyes and very quietly and calmly you will say, "Stay," as you stroke her.
2. Have her hold that position for thirty seconds while you move slowly around her and then return to her side and give her lots of praise. Do that over and over again until her length of staying time is three minutes.

Approach #3

Approach #3 is actually practice without practice. For example, you take her for a walk and you come to an automatic-sit. You give her the hand signal and tell her to stay.

1. Instead of moving in front of your dog, stand next to her in the heel position.
2. Give her the hand signal and tell her to stay.
3. Pause for a moment staying in the heel position.
4. Give her the hand signal again.

Approach #4

You will do the same as Approach #2 except you feed your dog treats continuously.

1. Begin at five-second intervals. Give her a treat.
2. Build up to ten-second intervals. Give her a treat.
3. Continue until she stays for a few minutes and you are giving her treats every so often.
4. You want to wean her off the treats as soon as possible.

Introducing Distractions

While working on the stay and lengthening the time, you can introduce distractions. Start with mild distractions such as tossing a pebble or a set of keys. Build up to things like toys, treats, and the most difficult one being bringing her out in public. Practice working on the stay in front of a supermarket. Inevitably, a person will walk by and squeal, "Oh, my gosh, what a beautiful dog! I must pet your dog. She is so beautiful." That is the biggest distraction and the one for which all dogs are praised—not by you of course—but by the well-intentioned person who is fawning all over your gorgeous girl.

Perfecting Distance

After two or three days of practicing the stay with distractions, you will be able to start building your distance. Make sure your dog is good at staying for three minutes with distractions on the short leash. Once she can do that, then put the long leash on her and start

Now I use the twenty-foot leash to work on even greater distance. Photo by www.mortonimages.com.

Reilly has shifted his weight, signaling he wants to get up. I move into him, gathering the leash, telling him in a calm voice to stay, and showing him the hand signal. Photo by www.mortonimages.com.

moving slowly farther and farther away from her while telling her to stay in a calm voice. Since keeping virtually no slack in the leash is more difficult with the twenty-foot leash, you will be relying on your voice and body language more to convince her to stay. If you see her ever so slightly shifting her weight or lowering her head—sure signs that she is about to pop up—move into her, shortening the leash as you go, calmly telling her to stay while you are showing her the hand signal. Before you know it, you can tell her to stay with your hand signal alone—no matter how far away you are.

Uncontrolled Distractions and Body Positioning

Now that you have worked on a steady stay with distractions, I want to explain what to do about natural, uncontrolled distractions when

Bonnie is not in a good position. Gordon and Ryan are the distraction. If Punky gets up to see them, Bonnie cannot stop him. Photo by Babette Haggerty-Brennan.

This is the correct position. If Punky runs to Gordon or the other dog, Bonnie can stop him. Photo by Babette Haggerty-Brennan.

Keeping Rocky between me and Isabella. Photo by www.mortonimages.com.

This is bad positioning. Baxter could wrap himself around my legs, tripping us both. Always walk to the right of the distraction. Photo by www.mortonimages.com.

you are out and about, such as a person walking his dog past you. This is where body positioning always comes in handy.

Always keep Ginger between you and the distraction. Most people when walking their dog, upon the sight of another dog will walk between their dog and yours. Big mistake! Their dog is cutting into them and going through their legs to get to you and your dog. They are losing control over the situation and could very well land on their tushies. You always want to walk to the right of the distraction. If you are walking to the right of the distraction, you are behind your dog and you are in a much better position to walk away from the distraction and get your dog's attention off the distracter.

Challenges Women Have Teaching the Sit-Stay

You are going to want to use your biceps to correct. That is a mistake. We tend to compensate for lack of upper-body strength by using our biceps, which is naturally the strongest muscle in the arm, whether one works out or not. You don't want to keep your arms bent. Your arms should be ready to be used to their fullest range of motion. You want to have maximum use of your arms, and if you are bending them and holding them tightly next to your body, several things are happening: (1) you are not relaxed; (2) your timing of a correction will be slow; and (3) you will expend more energy than necessary when you do administer a correction.

We use our sweet voices to seduce and get what we want from anyone, but if we use our voices incorrectly with our dogs, we have trouble. We have a higher pitch and longer range of voice tone. You will need to change your voice tone. If your dog starts to get up, use a deep tone and as you do that breathe in deeply and stand taller. The change in your body language will be enough for her to settle back into a sit. It is important that you speak softly and calmly. This is a relaxing exercise. It is important that if you are having a bad day or are very stressed you need to stay calm. If you are losing your patience, hang up the leash for the day.

Big boobies! Since when is that a curse? Now! If you are a lady who is extra blessed on top, you may not be able to move in as quickly to stop her with the leash. If you are "cursed" with big boobies, the best thing that you can do to compensate is make sure that your shoulders are relaxed and that you keep your feet shoulder-width apart. Do not stand straight and stuffy like a Buckingham Palace guard. Be relaxed and loose.

HOMEWORK

- Begin each practice session by reviewing what we have done up to this point.
- Build your dog up to a three-minute sit-stay next to you.
- Go to a public area where you can practice the sit-stay with your dog with distractions.
- As her sit-stay time increases, slowly increase your distance. If you are in an open area, do not drop the leash.
- Make sure she does a sit-stay before going through any door.
- When serving her food, make sure that she does a sit-stay while she waits.
- Practice for the next four days before progressing to the next lesson.

DAILY PRACTICE CHECKLIST

- Am I using a calm voice?
- Am I practicing when I am very hyper? Or am I calm?
- If I need to stop my dog from getting up, do I stop her before or after she gets up?
- When she lowers her head or shifts her weight, am I telling her to stay?

Lay Down, Sally

Don't waste your time hating a failure.

Failure is a greater teacher than success.

Listen, learn, go on.

—Clarissa Pinkola Estés

TOOLS NEEDED FOR TEACHING THE DOWN-STAY

training collar
five-foot leash
treats
twenty minutes

Imagine being able to bring Sally to the veterinarian's office and while you wait in the waiting room, you tell Sally to lie down. She does just that, even when the clinic dogs, Katie and Woody, come to visit. When I told Maria she would be able to do that with Gonzo, she was in shock. She didn't believe me until the day it happened. She called, "I am so excited. I brought Gonzo to doggy day care and while I waited for them to take him, I put him in a down-stay, and he did it!"

The biggest mistake that women make with this command is that they overuse and misuse the word *down*. For example, Sally jumps up on the couch, you say, "Down." She jumps up on your friends, you say, "Down." She jumps on the countertop, you say, "Down." Those are all situations and places in which she should learn to never ever jump, not even on Sundays.

This command is going to teach your dog to lie down and stay. This happens to be one of the more difficult commands to teach because it is a submissive command and a lot of dogs don't like to be in a vulnerable position. Do you? However, it is important that if you ask your dog to do something she will do it on your time, not hers. Who is the boss? She is, if you are changing your ways to fit her likes and dislikes, and accommodating your dog is a recipe for disaster.

The down-stay is very handy because it is less mobile than the sit-stay and if you put Sally in a down-stay, she will stay for a long period of time and is less apt to get up for distractions. It is also a very comfortable position.

There are also very handy applications to the down command. Imagine you are cooking Thanksgiving dinner for twenty and Sally is in the kitchen, and you want her to lie down and stay. She is going to learn to stay in a down position, food or no food, but she is also going to accept and tolerate you walking over her. You don't want to carry the bird from the oven and try to step over her as she gets up. You, Sally, and the bird will end up on the floor. We are going to

BELIEVE IT OR NOT!

I once attended an agility seminar at a local training club. There was a woman who had her Rottweiler with her. This woman was an active obedience and agility competitor. The conversation came up that Rottweilers don't like to be told to lie down or have people walk closely to them when they do lie down. I was dumbfounded. I have taught hundreds of Rottweilers to lie down. If you have a Rottweiler, you'd better teach her that if you want her to do something, she has to do it.

I saw this woman again last year at an obedience seminar with a Rottweiler. I don't know if it was the same dog, but this dog was temperamentally unsound. This woman's body language told me she was afraid of her own dog. When the woman told the speaker she didn't want to make her Rottweiler do the "retrieve" if her dog didn't want to do it, the speaker astutely picked up on it as well. If any breeder or trainer from whom you are considering purchasing a puppy tells you that, "XYZ breed doesn't like to do ABC," run awaaaay, as they say in *The Holy Grail*.

accustom your dog to being walked over. This is also handy if you have children running around the house; your dog will be used to feet coming toward her and she will sleep comfortably and not startle when little feet coming running and jumping over her. Carrying laundry and a baby have the same application.

Prepare for Success

Your dog must have a steady sit-stay before you begin teaching this command. She should be able to remain in a sit-stay for at least three minutes with distractions.

Breathing Exercises

Let's begin with our deep-breathing exercises.

1. Breathe in and count for four.
2. Exhale and count for four.
3. Repeat four times.
4. For the last breath make sure that you fill your lungs completely with air.
5. Completely empty your lungs.

Positive Visualization

Picture yourself on a Saturday afternoon. You picked Sally up from the groomer. You are running late and still have to get ready for your hot date tonight. As you sit in traffic, you look down and see that your bright red nail polish is all chipped. You went into the office this morning and you forgot about getting your nails done. There is no way you can go home, drop off Sally, go back to the nail salon, and get home in time for your date. You refuse to go out with your nails looking like that either. What is a girl to do? Take Sally and go to the first salon you see. You can't leave her in the car so you tie Sally to the post outside on the sidewalk. You say, "Down-stay." You go in and are able to get a manicure immediately. The entire half hour you are in there, you watch Sally lying down and staying—even for all the nice people who come to say hello to her, including the little barking terrier that ran past. Now it is time to leave. Sally is so happy to see you and you are so proud of her. And your nails look great.

Positive Affirmation

Close your eyes. I want you to repeat the following affirmation six times: "I can do this. I will do this. I can and will do this well."

Katas

As with the other commands, before we teach them to your dog, we are going to train you first. I want you to do this exercise, which I call the waist reducer, so that you can get used to the action without thinking about Sally just yet. It may seem odd, but believe me, once you practice this, Sally will learn to go down like a charm in just a few repetitions. You will be more confident and be able to focus on what Sally needs to do, instead of what you need to do. Now I will warn you that in many of my classes I have seen owners have a look of disbelief on their faces when I ask them to do this. In January 2001, exactly six nights before I gave birth to my child, I did this exercise in front of eighteen new students. If I could do it—and I was gargantuan—you can do it too. Make sure that you are wearing comfortable shoes and clothes for this exercise and now follow these steps:

1. Breathe in and out.
2. Place your feet a little more than shoulder-width apart.
3. Raise your left arm straight up.
4. Bring it down in front of you toward the left.
5. Bend your left knee and put all of your weight on your left side.
6. Touch the ground with the palm of your hand.
7. Make sure that your hand is flat down on the ground.

Repeat these steps seven to eight times. Make sure that when you perform this exercise, you do so in one continuous, fluid motion. You don't want to go up and down before touching the ground, just go all the way down. That was very good. Now that you have completed this exercise, go ahead and round up Sally. Put the leash on her and let's take her outside.

Here we go, girls! Big stretch! Photo by Babette Haggerty-Brennan.

All the way down to the left. Photo by Babette Haggerty-Brennan.

Make sure that your weight is on your left leg and that your palm is flat on the ground. Photo by www.mortonimages.com.

Approach #1

Just as you have warmed up, let's warm up Sally. Let's do some heeling, an automatic-sit, and at least two to three sit-stays.

1. Place Sally into a sit-stay.
2. Stay on her right side in the heel position.
3. Turn facing her.
4. Keep the leash in your right hand.
5. Keep the leash somewhat taut.
6. Place your feet shoulder-width apart.
7. Place your left hand six inches above her head.
8. Your palm should face down.
9. Slowly come down past her face with your left hand.
10. Slide your left hand under her muzzle.
11. Put the palm of your hand on top of her collar.
12. Apply minimal pressure.
13. As you do that, take your right hand and gently pull her left forequarter (her outside leg) out in front of her. This allows her to be off

The leash is taut but not too tight. I place my hand above Baxter's head so he can simultaneously learn the hand signal. Photo by www.mortonimages.com.

Bringing my hand down on top of the leash with my palm on the collar. Photo by www.mortonimages.com.

Gently lift the outside leg, breaking his balance. Photo by www.mortonimages.com.

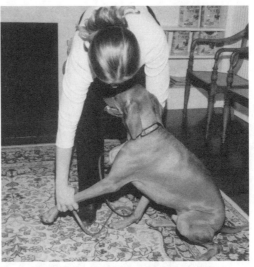

Maxwell is gently placed into position as I lift his outside leg and lean into him. Photo by www.mortonimages.com.

I don't let up until Baxter is all the way down.
Photo by www.mortonimages.com.

Since my hand is right next to Baxter's neck and ear, I start stroking him and praising him as soon as his elbows hit the ground. Photo by www.mortonimages.com.

balance. You are then placing her into position. Think of a table with a missing leg. It is off balance. You can easily tip it over by leaning into it.

14. Place her into the down. Put the back of your hand on her shoulder. Now slowly slide the back of your hand along her body and rub her side. She will slowly relax and roll away from you, showing you her belly. At this point, you are setting her up to teach her "on your back" as a separate command while praising at the same time.

15. Give her lots of praise, but do not fuss all over her with lots of exuberance. Tell her very softly and calmly that she is the best good girl

Maxwell automatically relaxes on his back because the back of my hand is a softer touch than the palm of my hand. Photo by www.mortonimages.com.

in the world. Stroke her softly. If you praise her this way, she will be calmer and more likely to stay in that position. If you get excited she will jump all over the place, absolutely thrilled with herself, and it will teach her that as soon as she goes down, she can pop back up. Just love her and stroke her softly.

Teaching the down in this way is very important. By using a minimal amount of "compulsion," we don't give her an opportunity to learn that she can choose not to do it. Yet, we are setting her up to succeed immediately, and not giving her the chance to fail. Be very careful to not resist the downward motion when you are prompting the collar down. If you resist, she will also learn to resist.

Q&A

As soon as I start to go down, she brings her rear end up. What's wrong?

Her stay is not steady enough. You need to do two things: (1) improve her stay, and (2) each time she rears up, tell her no and put her back into a sit position.

She is so strong. Am I not strong enough to get her to do this?

A lot of women think that strength plays an important part in training. It is not strength. It is using your center, your body, and your attitude. Women do lack the upper-body strength that makes this command easier for men to teach, so you want to use leverage to compensate for this. Make sure you are standing over her. Your center should be over her head and shoulders, not in front. Do not crouch down with her. Bend over her.

She rolls over on her back once she goes down. Is this OK?

OK? This is excellent! Great! Once she is on her back, softly rub her belly with just your fingertips, very lightly, and say, "On your back." Belly rubs are the ultimate praise for any dog, better than liver. You are also preparing her for the on your back command. If she rolls over, you have a bonus. You praise her in the best way possible. She loves it and you start on a new command.

Correct position: Ava has balance and leverage as she leans into Chesterfield. Photo by Babette Haggerty-Brennan.

Incorrect position: Ava is not balanced. Balance, leverage, and equilibrium—three important ingredients to training. Photo by Babette Haggerty-Brennan.

Approach #2

If your dog responds well to treats in training, try this approach. As always, as soon as she starts responding, start weaning her from the treats.

1. Take a treat or a toy.
2. Hold the leash in your left hand with her on your left.
3. Use your right hand to hold the treat or toy.
4. Bring your right hand down past her face.
5. Bring your right hand back toward her neck so that she has to tuck in her muzzle.
6. Place your right hand between her forequarters to the ground.
7. Move your hand forward toward her paws. You must do this very slowly.
8. Do *not* give her the treat or the toy until both of her elbows are on the ground.
9. Give her lots of calm and soothing praise.

Rocky is interested in the treat. Photo by Gordon Brennan.

Slowly I lure Rocky with the treat. Photo by Gordon Brennan.

I am holding the treat until Rocky is all the way down on his elbows. Photo by Gordon Brennan.

I give Rocky his well-deserved treat. Photo by Gordon Brennan.

I tell Rocky in a quiet voice that he is a good dog and I gently stroke him in his favorite spots. Photo by Gordon Brennan.

Q&A

As soon as she sees the treat or smells it, she grabs it out of my hand. Help!

Hold the treat in a tight fist. Do not allow her to take it until she is down on the ground and relaxed.

Once I give her the toy, she takes off with it and I can't get her back. Help!

I wouldn't use the toy as a reward until she learns to come to you when you call her. Otherwise, she is learning to take off on you and she is winning, which is not good.

She bites my hand so hard that I bleed. What can I do?

I wouldn't use this approach. Try another. However, when she does bite, make sure that you tell her no.

She puts her head down and looks at my hand. Why won't she lie down?

She may not be motivated by treats. You can also coax her along by pulling one of her forequarters out, preferably the one she is leaning on.

THE BIRTH OF PUPPY PUSH-UPS

In the summer of 1994 I went to California and spent the summer with my dad. We spent the summer training and showing dogs. We were working with a girl's Basenji. The dog had a hyperactivity problem. My dad had the dog doing repeated sits and downs, over and over again. He was showing the dog's owner how to do these exercises quickly before she left the house in the morning and in the evening before and after her training homework to decrease the dog's destructiveness. In the middle of these fast repetitions, I said, "Puppy push-ups." My dad smiled. That November I was at the very first dog trainers' conference of its kind in Orlando, Florida. A trainer from New Jersey was asking my dad for some training advice. He started giving her some ideas. I interjected and said, "Puppy push-ups." He smiled, remembering our past summer and the Basenji. A year later, this same trainer spoke at the Association of Pet Dog Trainers (APDT) conference and recommended puppy push-ups in her speech. Since then it has become a popular term and technique when training dogs. Practicing these push-ups will tire an active dog and decrease the destructiveness in those dogs that chew and destroy. Even more importantly, puppy push-ups will help tune up your dog's promptness and timing on sits and downs.

Perfecting the Down-Stay

Once she is good at the down, start her on the down-stay command. This is almost identical to the sit-stay command:

1. Put her into a down.
2. Give her the hand signal.
3. Turn and stand in front of her.
4. Proceed to walk around her.

Stepping over Your Dog

It is very important that you teach your dog to tolerate being walked over. You want to be able to step over your dog without her getting up, which could cause you both to fall down. Remember to visualize yourself successfully carrying that Thanksgiving turkey across the kitchen as you step over Sally while she's lying down. Follow these steps to accustom Sally to being walked over:

1. Put her in a down-stay.
2. Start walking over her from the rear to the front. It is important that you start from the rear first because she is less likely to get up than if you move toward her.
3. Say, "Stay," in a very low, quiet tone.
4. Walk over her from the rear first, five times in a row.
5. Once she is accepting of that, walk over her from the side, while you say, "Stay." Do that at least five times.
6. Alternate practicing walking over her from the side and from the rear.
7. Once she is nice and steady, then practice stepping over her from the front. If she starts to get up as you approach her from the front, quietly say, "No, stay," and make sure you are showing her the hand signal.
8. At this point, you can stand in front of her and just take your foot and bring it over her head, back and forth. Do this half a dozen

Isabella stays while I walk over her.
Photo by www.mortonimages.com.

Isabella is now used to being walked over, so now I walk toward her face first. Photo by www.mortonimages.com.

times, and this will get her used to your feet coming toward her face.

9. In one or two practice sessions, she will have succeeded at this simple skill. Repeat this over and over until she becomes steadier.

Down-out-of-Motion

This command is a variation of the automatic-sit and is quite handy. It actually has a military application to it. When soldiers are in combat and they need to duck from sudden fire, so do their dogs: boom—hence the down-out-of-motion. This command will really sharpen Sally's skills and make her focus on you even more. Follow these steps:

1. Start heeling.
2. Slow down your pace.

3. Slide your left hand down the leash toward her and say, "Down."
4. Apply a little pressure downwards.
5. Let her up right away and take another step.
6. Take a few more steps together and repeat.

If you do this three to four times a practice session, she will improve considerably after the first session.

Typically, I recommend taking a step forward—boom, down-out-of-motion, take another step forward, and another down-out-of-motion, then one more step and down again. If you do this "tapping of the brakes" once in the beginning, middle, and end of your practice sessions you will have a dog that is very focused on you and really tighten up her obedience.

HOMEWORK

- Start your practice with some heeling exercises.
- Work on an automatic-sit.
- Do the automatic-sit. Take one step and have her sit again. Take another step and have her sit again. Take a third step and have her sit one more time.
- You can move onto the sit-stay. If she goes into the down, I wouldn't worry about it.
- Practice the down each day.
- Build her up to a five-minute down-stay.
- Build distractions such as a treat thrown in front of her. You will then increase the intensity of the distractions by introducing bigger distractions, such as bicyclists going past. Remember that you want to keep her between you and the distraction—the bike rider. If she gets up, correct her by heeling her *away* from the distraction.
- Walk over her. Start from the rear first. She is more apt to get up if you walk toward her rather than straddle her.
- Repeat this several times.
- Now start walking over her from the front first. (Remember this will prepare you for Thanksgiving Day.)
- Once she is good at that, move on to puppy push-ups.
- Do ten in a row.
- Practice the down-out-of-motion.

Kaiser knows to remain in the down-stay while the bike rider passes us. Photo by Gordon Brennan.

Lara is nicely balanced with her left foot on the leash. Photo by Babette Haggerty-Brennan.

Lara is not balanced with her right foot on Dario's leash. Photo by Babette Haggerty-Brennan.

- You want to do the down-out-of-motion immediately before your practice, in the middle of it, and at the end.
- If you run into a friend and want to stand a bit and talk, put Sally into a down-stay on your left side and put your left foot onto the leash. You want to use your left foot because if she gets up, she will correct herself. If you put your right foot on the leash, you will not be as balanced and she can throw you off if she gets up.

DAILY PRACTICE CHECKLIST

- Am I using a soft tone?
- Am I using praise too exuberantly on the stay causing Sally to get up?
- Am I staying relaxed?
- Am I practicing with a positive attitude?
- Do I make sure I have my hand close to her neck when I apply pressure down?
- If she resists, do I stop?

Keep up the good work and before you know it, you will look like this great class of students in their fourth week of basic.

The result of practicing. Group class, week four: practicing three-minute sit-stays and five-minute down-stays. Photo by Babette Haggerty-Brennan.

Come on, Eileen

Dogs come when they're called;

cats take a message and get back

to you.

—*Mary Bly*

**TOOLS NEEDED FOR
TEACHING THE COME
COMMAND**

training collar
five-foot leash
twenty-foot leash
(small dogs)
thirty-foot leash
(large dogs)
twenty minutes

When Jennie called me to train her Golden Retrievers, it was very important to her that the dogs would come when called. She lives on a very busy main street. If the dogs ever got out and didn't come when called, they would be killed instantly.

I think the easiest command for a woman to teach a dog is to come when called. Our naturally higher-pitched voices make any dog want to come to us. Since we are generally smaller than men and more naturally use body language, we are less threatening to a dog. Dogs will not come to you if they are afraid of you. Some will submissively crawl over to you, but we want to teach Eileen that when we say, "Come," she stops on a dime and comes. She needs to come the first time we call her. A truly trained dog doesn't need to be told more than once.

Prepare for Success

You can't expect to have success without preparing for it first.

Breathing Exercises

Go to a quiet place. Remember that your breaths should be slow and deliberate.

Take your time. The purpose is to calm you:

1. Inhale as much air as you can.
2. Exhale all of it out of your lungs.
3. Relax your shoulders.
4. Repeat until you are relaxed.

Positive Visualization

Pretend that you and Eileen are at the dog park. The dogs are romping and playing. It is the usual big party. Of course, Eileen is having the time of her life. She is in a locked play position with three other dogs. They are all rolling around completely oblivious to the world around them. You are watching from about fifty yards away while chatting with friends. The next thing you know, you look at your watch and you realize you were supposed to pick your granddaughter up from school twenty minutes ago and you are fifteen minutes away from her school. You call out, "Eileen! Come!" She wastes no time. You see her roll out of the play position, jump up on all four, shake herself off, and come running. The other dogs are chasing and jumping on her. She ignores them with the look of "My mommy just called me. Leave me alone. I have to go. See you tomorrow."

Positive Affirmation

Close your eyes. I want you to repeat the following affirmation six times: "I have the best dog. She is perfect. She will come to me when I call her under any circumstance. I am going to have a lot of fun teaching this command because it is simple."

Katas

Let us first learn the whirling hairball, which is the kata we use to teach the come command.

1. Stand tall with your left arm straight out to the side.
2. Bring your left hand to your right shoulder.
3. Do this three times.

Excellent! Now we are going to add to this:

4. Stand tall with your left arm straight out to the side.
5. Bring your left hand to your right shoulder.
6. As you do this, start turning to your right.
7. You want to turn a full 360 degrees.
8. When you finish turning, you should be facing the same direction in which you started.
9. Your left hand should still be on your right shoulder.
10. Repeat this three times.

Good job! Now let's make sure that we have comfortable shoes on and the short leash on Eileen. Bring the long leash outside with you.

My arm is straight out to the side. Photo by www.mortonimages.com.

I bring my left hand to my right shoulder. Photo by www.mortonimages.com.

Everyone can do the whirling hairball. Photo by Babette Haggerty-Brennan.

We are not dizzy yet! Photo by Babette Haggerty-Brennan.

Approach #1

As always, now that you have warmed up, we want to warm up Eileen to prepare her for learning. Start with a series of automatic-sits. Heel for a few minutes. Do a three-minute sit-stay and follow with more heeling. Do a down-stay for five minutes and follow with more heeling. Practice the down-out-of-motion three times and follow with more heeling. Finish the warm-up by putting Eileen in a sit-stay.

Stage #1

We are going to teach the come command in three stages. For the first two stages, we will use the five-foot leash. To begin, follow these steps:

1. Place Eileen into a sit-stay.
2. Walk to the end of the leash.
3. Turn and face her.
4. Put your left thumb through the loop.
5. Put your left arm out to the side.
6. Call Eileen in a happy tone, "Eileen, come!"
7. Bring your left hand to your right shoulder.
8. As you bring it to your right shoulder, start backing up and turning to the right 360 degrees.

Cano waits for his command. Photo
by Gordon Brennan.

Cano has been distracted, but he
still has to come when I call him.
Follow through with the process
despite the distraction. Photo by
Gordon Brennan.

I bring my left hand to my right
shoulder. Photo by Gordon Brennan.

I start to back up as he comes closer,
making him come to me more quickly.
Photo by Gordon Brennan.

As I turn, I am maintaining balance by
keeping my feet shoulder-width apart.
Photo by Gordon Brennan.

Even a pregnant woman can keep up with a Mastiff like Cano, owned and loved by St. Louis Cardinal Johnny Hernandez. Photo by Gordon Brennan.

Cano is coming around to my left, and I am verbally praising him in the process. Photo by Gordon Brennan.

Cano sits and I tell him that he is a great dog, while I love and physically praise him. Photo by Gordon Brennan.

9. Eileen will end up on your left side.
10. Have her sit.
11. Give lots of praise.

As she comes to you, remember to encourage her along, giving lots of praise: "Good girl, come on, good girl. That is my sweetheart." Practice this ten times.

Stage #2

Now that she is coming to you, you want to stop having to turn. You want her to come and place herself at your left side once you call her.

1. Place her in a sit-stay.
2. Walk to the end of the leash.
3. Face her.
4. Put your left thumb through the loop.
5. Say, "Eileen! Come, good girl."
6. Bring your left arm to your right shoulder.

Both LuLu and Monty are giving and receiving lots of love for a job well done.
Photo by www.mortonimages.com.

7. She will come to you on the right, circle around you, and end up on your left side.
8. Once she sits, fuss all over her, and give her tons of praise. Love her all over.

Good job! Before we progress to Stage #3, I would like for you to practice these steps ten times.

Stage #3
This time you are going to put your long twenty- or thirty-foot leash on Eileen. Allow her to walk around wherever she wants to smell

Reilly is distracted when I call him. Photo by www.mortonimages.com.

I back up and praise Reilly as he comes toward me. Photo by www.mortonimages.com.

the flowers and grass. Now we are ready to begin the third stage. Follow these steps:

1. Go to *almost* the end of the leash.
2. Once she is distracted and doing something else, call her, "Eileen, come."
3. Give the leash a tug. From this distance she will feel a light pull, which will be enough to get her attention. She will learn that the first time you call her is when she must drop everything and come running.
4. As she comes toward you, start running backwards.
5. As soon as she gets to you, give her lots and lots of praise.

Approach #2

Now being a dog trainer is tantamount to having many tricks up your sleeve. Tools can be used in all sorts of unorthodox ways. When a famous musician and her family in Palm Beach asked me to help them to teach their dogs to come when called, the housekeeper wanted me to train the dogs to come to the clicker. The housekeeper's job was to walk the dogs early in the morning. The dogs were walked beneath the owners' bedroom window, and since she had to walk the dogs before the owners woke up, the housekeeper didn't want to wake them by calling the dogs. Moreover, they were on the ocean, and it was sometimes hard for the dogs to hear her call if the wind was blowing hard. We decided to teach the dogs to come to the sharp sound of the clicker; however, we decided we would also teach them to respond to the voice command, along with the hand signal. The way we are going to use the clicker is different than the clicker training that is normally used. We are not going to fade out the clicker; the clicker is going to become the command. For example, instead of saying, "Come," we are going to click. Now let's try this with Eileen:

1. Let Eileen run around on the long leash.
2. Click the clicker and reel her into you.
3. Give her lots and lots of praise.
4. Repeat this four to five times. Each time you will lengthen your distance from Eileen.

After you do this five times in a row, you will find that she will stay close.

Another great practice exercise for Eileen is walking her through the park. Tell her to go ahead and let her run ahead of you. As soon as she is almost to the end of the leash, twenty-nine feet, call her to you or give a click. When she returns to you, be sure to praise her all over. Give her rubdowns up and down along her sides. Massage her ears. You will find that when you walk through the park with her, she will start to run ahead of you and simply turn around and come back to you just as she is about twenty-nine feet ahead of you. She will begin to do this automatically. This is great because it accomplishes two things:

1. She learns to stay within a certain distance of you.
2. She gets double the exercise in less time, making your life easier.

Q&A

My dog starts coming to me before I call her. What do I do?

Go back and increase your sit-stays. She is also learning to anticipate what you are going to do. Fool her a little. Place her in a stay, walk to the end of the leash, turn and look at her, then return to her side and lavish her with praise.

As soon as she gets close to me, she starts to back away. Why is this happening?

It sounds like you are not finishing the command. In other words, you are not having her circle around you to end up on your left side in a sitting position. Make sure that as she comes closer to you, you don't reach out to praise her. You shouldn't adjust yourself to her; she should adjust to you. As she moves closer, back up a little bit, and encourage her to come to you.

She comes halfway and then starts to chase a bird. What's a girl to do?

She has learned that she doesn't have to come to you the first time you call her. If she starts to take off in another direction, say, "No," give the leash a tug, start backing up, and reel the leash in to you. The entire time you should be sweetly calling her name.

Sometimes she comes right up to me and then attempts to take off. Do I follow her?

No. Make sure that you don't go to her to praise her. She must come all the way to you for praise. Also be sure that you never call her to you to discipline her for something.

This long leash is so hard to handle. Help!

I agree. It really is, but you can get used to it. Once you give her the signal and bring your left hand to your right shoulder, put your right thumb through the loop. Pull back on the leash with your right thumb allowing your left hand to guide it along as you pull it in closer to you.

HOMEWORK

- Practice the come command each day, twelve to fifteen repetitions.
- Make sure you praise her enthusiastically as she comes to you.
- Interchange all of the commands you have taught her thus far.
- Practice with distractions.

This group of students is remembering to keep their dogs between them and the distractions and not allowing the leashes to become entangled. Photo by Babette Haggerty-Brennan.

The owners are backing up as they call their dogs to them. Photo by Babette Haggerty-Brennan.

DAILY PRACTICE CHECKLIST

- Am I using a happy voice when I call Eileen to me?
- Am I backing up as she comes toward me?
- Am I using my hand signal consistently?
- Am I making sure that she comes right up to me before I praise her, or do I move into her?

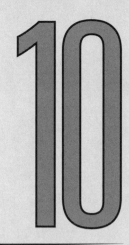

Movin' Out

I love to see a young girl go out and grab

the world by the lapels. Life's a bitch.

You've got to go out and kick ass.

—*Maya Angelou*

TOOLS NEEDED FOR TEACHING THE MOVE COMMAND

flat buckle collar
five-foot leash
five minutes

Mary called me telling me that when she brought her new baby, Johanna, home from the hospital she was having trouble with Peaches, her six-year-old Golden Retriever. Peaches would always sleep in front of the nursery door. Mary was still sore from childbirth and had a hard time carrying Johanna into the nursery because Peaches would just lie there and not move. So we decided to teach Peaches the move command to make things easier for Mary.

Not only is the move command extremely useful, but it is also very easy to teach. If you want to be more ladylike, you can say, "Excuse me," or "Pardon me," instead of saying, "Move."

There are several instances where you would use the move command in its various forms. For example, you are walking in the door carrying groceries and Peaches is there to greet you. You need to put the groceries down before petting her and she is blocking your path to the kitchen. You will say to her, "Pardon me," and she will

173

move. Now if you are in a real hurry, like running to the bathroom while she lies in the hallway, you need her to move quickly so you will say, "Move." Naturally, you are going to use a more urgent tone in your voice.

Teaching the Move Command

The move command is very easy to teach. Practice these steps with Peaches, and after three or four times, she will be moving:

1. Walk toward Peaches shuffling your feet.
2. As you move toward her, you are going to slightly raise your feet, almost like a march.
3. You just want to give her a gentle nudge with your toes.
4. As you are moving toward her, you want to say, "Move" (or "Excuse me" or "Pardon me") and point with your hand behind her.
5. Keep moving into her until she starts to get up.
6. As soon as she gets up, walk toward her a few more steps so she learns that she is to move away.
7. Give her lots of praise.

Q&A

What happened if she only sits on the move command?

That is OK. You haven't finished the movement. She doesn't know what you want yet. Keep moving toward her pointing in the direction behind her. She will understand what you want by your body language and move out of your way. Just keep moving toward her and she will get up.

You can also combine this with the raus command from the next chapter. The difference between raus and move is that you want her to move away while you are moving toward her. The raus is when you send her away. The raus is more difficult to teach because you are standing still, not moving toward her, so she thinks you don't want her to move away.

Why don't you suggest using a treat for this command?

I want Peaches to move *away* from me, not *to* something. It's a very mild difference and for the average dog owner it makes no sense, but to your dog there is a huge difference. If you were to train her by throwing a treat past her, she will jump up (if she is motivated by food), look for it, and if for some reason she cannot find the treat or she eats it and wants another, she will come back toward you looking for more. You don't want her doing that. We want her to move on out. We want her to keep moving away as if she has a place to go—dogs to see or fire hydrants to sniff.

HOMEWORK

- Warm up by reviewing all of the commands you and your dog have learned thus far.
- Practice doing various commands throughout each day. For example, place your dog in a sit-stay at the front door.
- As soon as your dog is doing the move command three times in a row, you can progress to teaching the raus command in the next chapter.

DAILY PRACTICE CHECKLIST

- Do I keep moving into her or do I stop?
- Am I pointing where I want her to go as I repeat the command?
- Do I repeat the command over and over so that she hears what I want her to do?

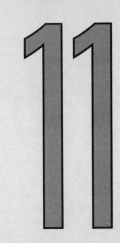

"Raus" Rhymes with "House"

> *There is a potential heroine in*
>
> *every woman.*
>
> —Jean Shinoda Bolen

"**D**aisy can't come to class tonight. I was cooking last night and I dropped a glass. She came running in and stepped on the glass cutting her foot. I had to take her to the emergency room. The veterinarian said that she has to stay in her crate. It is awful. She cries, cries, and cries."

That was the beginning of the long-winded message left on the voice mail one day. Daisy's mom, owner Liza, hadn't done two important things with Daisy: (1) she hadn't practiced teaching Daisy the "raus" command, and (2) she never properly crate-trained her.

"What the heck is 'raus'? What does crate-training have to do with anything?" Good questions, Fraulein!

The raus command is actually from *voraus*, which is a command in the German-originated sport of SchutzHund that means to send away. The Germans will say "raus" like a contraction. It isn't rude, but it can be interpreted as not the most polite way to talk to someone.

On one of my trips to Germany, my husband who speaks no German was in the backseat of the hatchback I was driving. Frau Diener, a very nice lady with whom I lived for a summer, speaks less English than my husband speaks German. I pulled up to a restaurant and told my husband I would let them both out while I found a parking spot. Just as I was about to translate for Frau Diener, my husband called from the back seat, "Frau Diener, raus." She understood and got out. I was so embarrassed. My husband realized his faux pas and then apologized to her. She understood and fortunately wasn't offended. Saying "raus" isn't rude, but it is very commanding, and a man speaking to an elderly woman in a commanding tone isn't exactly appropriate.

If Daisy's mom had crate-trained her, Daisy wouldn't be crying in the crate while on crate rest. Not crate-training your dog is a terrible injustice. How will she feel if something happens and she has to stay overnight at the veterinarian's office or in this case has to be on crate rest? She will be confined there and if she is not used to it, you are making a stressful situation for her even more stressful. Get her used to the crate immediately. "Oh, I will never keep her at the vet's." I know you won't, willingly, but if she is ten years old, too sick to go home, and the vet insists that she be monitored overnight, it will be in her best interest to keep her there.

You understandably want to know what crate-training has to do with the raus command. Well, remember, we need a foundation to training—these things are all interrelated. Keep reading and be patient, and you will see shortly how the two are related.

Quick Visualization

Close your eyes and picture yourself as a shepherd herding a flock of sheep. You move to the right when they move to the right. If they move too far to the left, you go to their left and drive them back into position. You keep them between you and where you want them to go. This is the herding position.

Teaching the Raus Command

The raus command is tremendously useful in circumstances like Daisy's. It is also handy if you have the kind of dog that loves to follow you into the bathroom. Usually, you don't mind, but sometimes you just need to escape from the world, and we all know that the bathroom is the only place a girl can hide. If your Daisy follows you in there and you want her out, just say to her, "Daisy, raus." Well, how do you do it? It is easy. Just follow these steps:

1. Take a sandwich-sized brown paper bag.
2. Open it up.
3. Take a scant handful of uncooked rice.
4. Place the rice into the bag.
5. Make sure that there is air in it.
6. Twist it closed. You now have a "raus bag."
7. Tap yourself with the bag.
8. Walk into the kitchen. (You want to teach this command in the kitchen first because that is where you are most likely to use it, especially in an emergency.)
9. Put Daisy on a very short leash and place her between you and where you want her to go.
10. Take the raus bag and place it between you and her.
11. Tap her rump with it. Remember the herding position. That is exactly what you are going to do. Herd Daisy out the door or wherever you want her to go, keeping her between you and where you want her to go. Keep tapping her rump, saying, "Raus." She will most likely move quickly away from the bag and run out the door. Think of playing soccer; we keep the ball between us and where we want it to go. Keep the bag between you and Daisy.
12. Once she is out of the room, make sure you give her lots and lots of praise. If you do this exercise three times, you will realize you will no longer need the bag. Just say, "Raus," and out she goes. Very occasionally a dog will freeze and not move. If that is happening, make

I have Rocky on a short leash between me and where I want him to go. Photo by Gordon Brennan.

I keep tapping Rocky while repeating the raus command until he goes where I want him to go. Photo by Gordon Brennan.

The bag stays between Soupie and me. Photo by Gordon Brennan.

sure you have her facing the correct direction and that you are not in the heel position.

It is important that you teach the raus command before you teach the kennel command (we'll learn the kennel command later in this

WHAT IS SCHUTZHUND TRAINING?

SchutzHund is actually a sport. Some will foolishly tell you that it makes a dog mean. The literal translation of *SchutzHund* is "sport dog." Captain Max Von Stephanitz, the father of the German Shepherd Dog, wanted the breed to be the all-around dog. SchutzHund tests a dog's obedience, tracking ability, and protection training, also known as bite work. (One benefit of tracking is that the dog can find a missing person. Dogs that have been trained in search and rescue first had basic training foundation in tracking scent. These types of dogs have become more popular since 9/11.)

This test was formulated to measure a dog's overall skills in each area. Dogs that have received this self-rewarding training prove their breeding potential in this rigorous and demanding sport.

The sport demands nothing but the most temperamentally sound dog.

Why is Schutzhund training self-rewarding? Dogs love to use their nose and they get to do just that during the tracking test. Obedience training makes a dog happy, healthy, wealthy, and wise. Protection training—which is the most exciting to watch, in my opinion—gives the dog an opportunity to "play" tug-of-war. At any SchutzHund competition, the most heavily attended test is the bite work. Watching a dog run with such enthusiasm toward a "fleeing criminal" and take a flying leap to grab onto the "bad guy" is quite exciting. These dogs are very athletic and fear nothing. If you want a good, steady, even-tempered guard dog, you want a dog who has received a SchutzHund degree.

chapter) because we don't want Daisy to confuse "raus" and "kennel." If you teach her kennel before raus, she may start running toward her kennel when she leaves the room. With raus we want her to go anywhere—we don't care where—just go. Think of the joke of the Chinese buffet. The big eaters keep eating and eating and eating. The owner runs them out the door, saying, "You go now. Go now. You go now."

COMMON ERRORS
1. **Remaining in the heel position.** If you do this, you are not going to be effective in sending Daisy away.
2. **Standing between her and where you want her to go.** You can't herd her out the door if you are blocking the door.

Go to Your Kennel

Again, I urge you to incorporate crate-training into your dog's life. Dogs are natural pack animals and den animals, meaning their wild counterparts stay with a group of dogs and look for quiet, dark, closed-in spaces to find refuge. A dog that is crate-trained will be happy to be left home alone in her crate, will be easier to transport, and can be sent to her crate when there is company around. Whatever the reason you choose to utilize your dog's crate, you will need to remember that the crate should be considered a safe haven and a relaxing place, not the room you send your dog to when she's disobeyed you. *Never* use her crate as a form of punishment. OK, now that I've talked you into crate-training, here is the concept, which is exactly the same as the raus technique, but this time you are going to stand about five to six feet from her kennel with the door open:

1. Place Daisy between you and the kennel.
2. Throw a treat into the kennel.
3. Tap Daisy's rump with the raus bag saying, "Kennel, kennel, kennel, kennel."
4. As soon as she gets in her kennel, allow her the treat and give her praise while she is *inside* the kennel.
5. Do this three to four times. She should have it down pat by then.
6. Don't forget with each progression, to move farther and farther away from the kennel.

IMPORTANT TIPS
1. If she starts to respond without the raus bag, then by all means stop using it.
2. You can call this command anything that you want: "Kennel," "Crate," "House," "Bed," or "Place."
3. If your dog stops moving, drop the bag, and scoot her with your feet.
4. If you played soccer in school, you will remember when kicking a soccer ball, you had to keep it in between your feet, in front of you, while you moved it forward. You can scoot her forward as you would a soccer ball.

Drop It

*There are no problems—only
opportunities to be creative.*

Dorye Roettger

Claudine called me about her dog. "Our Standard Poodle has bitten a toad three times. The vet said that if she ever gets one again, she will die. Is this something that we can correct?"

Buffo toads and snakes are just a few of the wild animals that can kill our dogs. One lick of a poisonous buffo toad's skin and your dog can die very quickly and painfully. One bite from a poisonous snake and your dog can also die a terrible death. What we want to do is teach her to leave it/drop it.

It isn't really necessary to teach her both. We know there is a difference between leave it and drop it. *Leave it* means "don't touch it" whereas *drop it* means just that—"drop it." You can just teach one command and use it for the occasion before your dog picks something up or after she has it in her mouth.

This command is very simple to teach, and with regular practice after a few initial training sessions, your dog will have it down in no time flat.

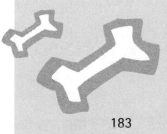

Visualize This

You are walking down the street and your dog picks up a chicken bone from an unknown mouth. Of course, you are completely grossed out and you don't want to touch it. You say, "Drop it." She drops it and you both keep on walking.

One Fast, Simple, Foolproof Approach

If you practice the following steps three to four times daily over the next couple of days, you will find that your dog will fully understand and reliably "drop it" every single time:

1. Put Valentine on a short leash and choker chain.
2. Get her favorite toy or a forbidden object.
3. Offer it to her.
4. Let her hold it in her mouth for three seconds.
5. Say, "Drop it."
6. Quickly snap the lead.
7. She will drop it.
8. Give her lots and lots of praise.
9. Try it one more time.
10. She may hesitate taking the object.
11. If she does, don't worry about it.
12. Try it with another object.
13. Repeat.
14. Give her lots and lots of praise.
15. Take her for a walk and throw an object ahead of you that you know she will want.
16. Once she starts going for it, say to her, "No, drop it," and snap the leash. If you do this correctly, she won't ever pick it up.

Drop it is probably the easiest and fastest command to teach. When dealing with objects, such as chicken bones or critters that could kill your dog, you don't have time to teach this any other way.

Let's Potty!

Failure is impossible.

—*Susan B. Anthony*

I have received so many calls over the years from people who had dogs that were not yet housebroken. Some have been as old as six years. I remember a lady with a six-year-old Cocker Spaniel that still wasn't house-trained even though she had gotten the dog as a pup. Now after six years of the dog destroying two carpets, the woman thought she might want to think about training. Not only did she want me to housebreak her dog, she wanted me to give her a guarantee and a discount as well. I laughed . . . to myself. She has already guaranteed me that she won't do what she needs to do and she wants it for less. That is like walking into triple bypass surgery and saying, "Hey, Doc. I am going to keep drinking and smoking and not exercise. Give me the works, guarantee me that I will live, and I want a discount to boot." Doc would do what I did: I sent her very politely elsewhere.

As soon as you get your dog—whether she's a puppy or an adult—buy her a crate. I recommend the airline type crate for the reasons I discussed in Chapter 3. You may hate the idea of the crate, but let me ask you this: Did you have a room of your own growing up? If you had to share, did you want your own room? How would you have felt if your parents said, "Oh, dear, for bed tonight, just find a spot to lie down somewhere"? The crate gives your dog a place of her very own. It is a place where she can escape and relax, a place where neither children nor the cat will bother her. She can chew and meditate on her bones in peace.

To accustom Diva to her crate, start by feeding her in there. Place all of her toys inside, along with her water and food. You want her to spend time in there enjoying the smells and her new bed. Now, use caution: if you are going to place her bed inside, make sure she doesn't use the bedding for a toilet. If you find that she is doing that, pull the bedding out immediately. I promise she will still be comfortable without a bed. The bottom of the crate is nice and cool so she will stay comfortable. Don't forget that even your Diva likes to lie in the dirt; dogs don't need 350-thread-count sheets like the movie stars.

Make sure that if she starts crying in the crate, you don't get suckered into letting her out. Otherwise, she will learn that all she has to do is cry and she will be let out.

Crate-Training

Crate-training serves many purposes. It basically means that Diva will learn to stay in her crate for extended periods of time. This will not only help you with house-training, but it can be used as a management and safety tool as well. Follow these steps to crate-train Diva successfully:

1. First thing in the morning take your dog out for five to seven minutes. She is out there to relieve herself, not to play.
2. Bring her inside and feed her in her crate. Leave the food down for only ten minutes. What she doesn't eat, pick back up, and save for dinner.
3. One half hour later, take her outside for five to seven minutes only.
   a. If she goes, let her run around the house for fifteen minutes.
   b. If she doesn't, return her to the crate.

4. Immediately before you leave, take her out again for five to seven minutes. If she doesn't go, don't worry. Go ahead and return her to the crate.

5. As soon as you return home, take her out again for five to seven minutes.
   a. If she goes, let her run around the house for fifteen minutes.
   b. If she doesn't, return her to the crate.

6. When you are at home, take her out every two hours.
   a. If she goes, let her run around the house for fifteen minutes.
   b. If she doesn't, return her to the crate.

7. Feed her no later than five hours before bedtime.

8. Continue taking her out through the evening. If she doesn't go, go ahead and return her to the crate.

9. The last walk in the evening should be a ten-minute brisk walk to give her the opportunity to completely empty herself. Tuck her in the crate, kiss her good night, and turn out the lights.

   Over time you will not have to take her out as often. You will also give her more free time around the house—after she has gone to the bathroom outside.

Don't think that you have to take Diva out throughout the night. You don't want to establish that habit. As long as you keep her in a dark, quiet area to sleep, she will make it through the night. If you start setting your alarm to go off at night, Diva's body will become accustomed to you and her getting up, and I doubt that you want to get up each night several times for the next fifteen years.

It is important to understand that young puppies cannot hold it for long periods of time. See the chart that follows for general guidelines. Be fair to your dog and don't make her hold it for extended periods of time.

Puppies two to four months	Take out every two to three hours.
Puppies four to six months	Take out every three to four hours.
Puppies six to nine months	Take out every four to six hours.
Dogs nine months and up	They can hold it up to eight hours.

Q&A

Even though my dog isn't completely crate-trained yet, I feel terrible keeping her confined to her crate all the time.

While you are crate-training her, you can let her out of her crate occasionally by employing the "cheating method" as discussed in the next answer.

I don't want to crate-train her. Can't I do something else?

OK, I'll admit it. We can cheat. It's easy. Instead of keeping her in the crate, take her leash and tie it to your belt loop on your left side or around your waist so that she is in the heel position. Let her stay with you. This way she will be with you, and she can't sneak off to go to the bathroom. You will also learn her "I gotta go potty" signal more quickly. While she is tied to you, you should still be taking her outside regularly.

I call this method of house-training the cheating method, but this works even better than crate-training because you are constantly with Diva, and indirectly she is getting her obedience practice in as well. For example, you are sitting at your computer writing a soon to be best-seller, just like me, and Diva is attached to you lying at your side. You have reinforced this down-stay by telling her to stay. Voilà! You are practicing while not having to make the time to practice.

My Yorkie is one year old. Can she still be housebroken?

Ugh, I hate these calls. I feel bad for the owner and the dog. I emphatically let them know that it is a superbly difficult job. It is important that if your dog is old, you must, absolutely, beyond a shadow of a doubt, to the letter, follow the program exactly and not deviate in the slightest bit. Yorkies as well as other toy dogs can be difficult to house-train. If your toy breed is not house-trained by four months of age, get professional help immediately!

The guy at the store told me not to feed her in her crate. Did I hear right?

I am not sure where that silly rumor started, but if you feed Diva in the crate, she will associate it with something wonderful.

My dog goes to the bathroom in her kennel, and I was told she would never go in her kennel.

You are correct in theory. Most dogs are not willing to go in the same area in which they eat and sleep, but assess the situation: Is she going to the bathroom in the bedding and then pushing it to the side? Is she rolling around in her mess? Is she eating it?

If she is going to the bathroom on the bed and pushing it off to the side, she does not have "dirty dog syndrome." She does this because she can relieve herself while keeping herself clean. If this is the case, make sure that you pull the bedding out; otherwise, she will continue to dirty her bed. Going to the bathroom in her area is not offensive to her as long as she can roll it up and push it to the side.

If Diva is rolling or lying in her mess and/or eating it, then she has "dirty dog syndrome." If this is the case, you'll want to house-train your dog according to the instructions in the section that immediately follows.

Help! I Have a Dirty Dog. What Is a Girl to Do?

Don't despair; help is here. You have to use a reverse house-training process. What this means is that instead of keeping Diva in the crate for extended periods of time, you will keep her outside for extended periods of time where she can relieve herself. This takes away the opportunity from her to have accidents in the crate.

You will want to keep Diva in a safe place outdoors. A grassy, shaded fenced-in area in your yard is ideal, or a secure, screened-in patio will work too. Once she relieves herself, she goes into the crate for a short period of time, the time that would normally be "free time." Don't worry: she will not view this as a punishment.

If you don't have a safe place for her to stay outside for periods of time, keep her leash tied to your belt loop instead of using the crate for confinement and take her outside every half hour. If you live in a walk-up, you are not as lucky, but you certainly will be skinnier. After all, think of how many more cuties you will meet if you are getting skinnier and walking more frequently. You will also be able to work more on your obedience training because you'll be practicing that many more sit-stays in the doorway. It is still important that you keep feeding her in the crate as well. Remember to only keep her in areas outside that are safe and secure from children teasing her, other animals that may harm her, or even people who may want to steal her.

Gross Me Out! Gag Me with a Spoon!

Some "dirty" dogs not only poop in their crates but will eat their business too. Your Diva is not that gross. She is a dog. Dogs are survivalists. Emily Post didn't tell them poop eating was socially unacceptable. Dogs behave on instinct.

Now if she is merely pooping in the crate, make sure that you are taking her out often enough. If Diva is actually eating her business, you want to make sure that she is getting a quality vitamin supplement. Many times dogs will eat Le Poop not just because it is a delicacy but also because they are lacking certain vitamins and minerals in their diets.

You can also get a product called Forbid from your veterinarian or try Accent meat tenderizer. Sprinkle either on her food. That may help.

Paper-Training

When Mrs. Jackson called me, she told me in her sweet Southern drawl that she wanted to paper-train Sugar, her Toy Poodle. She traveled often between Palm Beach and Boston. Her apartment in Boston was across the street from a park, but during a storm she didn't really want to have to go across the street to walk Sugar. I told her given Sugar's age of ten weeks, it would be easy. Incidentally, if you have an older toy dog that is still not house-trained, paper-training may be a good option for you.

We found a very small powder room that Mrs. Jackson didn't use often. If you don't have a separate room, you can simply block off a small area in your bathroom or kitchen. Instead of wall-to-wall carpet, Diva's new apartment will be wall-to-wall newspaper. There will be a small spot for her bed and water dish. The only place that she will relieve herself will be on newspaper. After all, that is all that is on the floor. How can she go anywhere else? Over time, you will start making the paper area smaller, one small sheet at a time.

If Diva goes on a non-papered area, immediately go back to putting more paper down. Keep going until Diva only goes to the papered area. Give it time, persistence, and patience. She will learn it well. However, don't make the mistake of starting her on newspapers with the thought that once she is older you will then house-train her. Putting papers down will teach her that it is OK to do it in the house.

I remember doing that with Lucy, another Toy Poodle, and her mother was ecstatic. "We took her to France and as soon as we put paper down for her in the bathroom, she went. She didn't even care that it was all in French."

Just Do It!

When Maxine called me about Delilah, she asked if we could train her Pomeranian to go to the bathroom on command. "I have an apartment in New York City, and it is a nuisance to take her across the street to the park during a blizzard for her to sniff around taking her time to go to the bathroom."

There is nothing more convenient than teaching your dog to do her business on command. If you live in a city where you must walk your dog instead of letting her out in the yard, it can be difficult when it is raining and snowing to have your dog sniff and sniff and sniff until she finds a suitable spot. The do your business command encourages her to go in an expeditious fashion. This also happens to be very easy to teach. Let's take Diva outside:

1. Allow her to sniff.
2. As she sniffs and circles, say, "Do your business," "Go make," "Let's potty," or whatever else you would like to call it.
3. As soon as she starts to relieve herself, stop the verbal command.

4. It is not necessary to give her a treat. The reward is in the relief of having gone to the bathroom. Don't you feel better once you go to the bathroom? Sure you do.

Nutrition and House-Training

Nutrition plays an important role in house-training. Make sure Diva is on a puppy food that is low in sodium. Puppies need to drink a lot of water, and many commercial pet foods have high sodium content, which will make Diva drink more water, increasing her need to urinate. Make sure that the food's sodium level is not too high for your puppy. This is more common in the supermarket brand foods than the premium foods that use human grade ingredients. Moreover, dog foods that use animal by-products, which means the food consists of the clean parts of the animal carcass (necks, feet, and intestines), may increase bowel movement size and frequency.

Whatever method you use for your dog—crate-training, outdoor training, belt-loop training, paper-training—as long as you are patient and persistent, you will successfully house-train your dog. If you have a toy breed, I can't emphasize it enough: if she isn't nearly perfect by four months, get professional help. One big mistake people will often make is that they try paper-training, then crate-training, and back to paper-training. That only confuses the issue and the dog. Pick what is easiest for your lifestyle and know you can both do it.

She's Got Issues

> *The good Lord in his ultimate wisdom*
> *gave us three things to make life*
> *bearable: hope, jokes and dogs, but the*
> *greatest of these was dogs.*
>
> —*Robyn Davidson*

Issues. We all have them, some more than others. Dysfunction. It is hip to be dysfunctional. We no longer shun celebrities or neighbors who visit their therapists on a weekly basis. They put the "fun" in dysfunctional. Well dogs, just like humans, have issues too.

I was working with a German Shepherd Dog named Blitz whose owner, Kiki, had given me the privilege of training her last German Shepherd Dog (also named Blitz). Originally, Blitz was going to come for training when he was a young pup. Instead, Kiki decided to work with him for a bit. When the methods she was using weren't working, she called us. He was about seven months old and still intact (not neutered); she was planning on showing him. He was quite a beautiful specimen, and I knew that he was destined to become a show champion. While training him, we found him to be a hyper dog, much different from the last Blitz that she had gotten. Five months after training, we received a call from her. He was having a serious aggression issue. Quite shocked, we made an appointment to go to her home. Who greeted me at the door—if you could call it that—wasn't Blitz. It was Cujo. I was dismayed to see Blitz behaving the way he was. That was not the same dog we had trained five months prior. Since we were unable to get into the house, she brought him outside. Eventually, my old friend accepted me. Working with him, I was not only in shock that he was a different dog, but I couldn't take my eyes off of him either because I didn't know if he was going to knock me down and devour me.

I put Blitz on a rigorous behavior modification and holistic program using flower remedies, massage techniques, a different dog food, as well as other changes in his life. We jumped in with both feet. He needed to be straightened out quickly. Kiki had a small yard and needed to be able to walk Blitz on the bike path in Palm Beach. Yet, with his behavior it was much too dangerous for her, him, and every other Palm Beach citizen and dog.

Diligent, Kiki came to every group class our school held. I was able to work her and Blitz one-on-one while Susan, one of our trainers, taught the class. Blitz improved over time. I also recommended to Kiki to attend either a yoga or tai chi class so that she could find her "center" and be able to handle him better. She would understand momentum and how he could use his energy to overpower her. Each week Kiki reported improvement, and she improved in her handling skills. His lunging at other dogs decreased greatly over a month. One day she arrived with her enormous black German Shepherd Dog in her shiny, black Mercedes four-door sedan, and a new dog emerged from the car. He was relaxed, happy, and confident. I was surprised at his drastic transformation in the past week. When you put your hands on him, the tension wasn't there. She reported that Blitz was doing better, and I noticed that she looked better too. Having confided in me in the past that her daughter was in drug treatment—again—I asked her how her daughter was doing and complimented that she herself looked better. We made small talk about what she was doing to cope with her daughter's disease of addiction. "You look great, Kiki. I am really happy for you. I am shocked about Blitz. He is ten times better than last week." Both Susan and Ana, our great class instructors, were baffled by the transformation. Kiki then said, "Well, you know, I sent my husband of the last two years off again. I don't even know where—he had just disappeared—again. This past week, when he showed up again, I threw him out." She then revealed the trouble she had been having with him over the last few months. "Emotionally, I am done with him. Now the attorney can deal with him. I am done." As she was talking, she realized that Blitz was a new dog because the tension in the house was gone; she had let go of a circumstance and person she could not control. Her new mantra was the Serenity Prayer: "God, grant me the serenity to accept the things I cannot change; courage to change the things I can; and the wisdom to know the difference." "You know, Babette," she said, "if I had remembered that prayer when I was going through it, I would have thrown him out more quickly. Now I know what Blitz was trying to tell me. Thank God that I have Blitz. He is the only man I need."

Fortunately for Blitz, Kiki was willing to work through his "issues" before giving up and throwing him out. If your dog is having "issues," I hope that you will be able to work through them. Something I have learned in life is that most often our problem with our dogs is us. If you are having a serious challenge with your dog, think about what is going on in your life and figure out how your dog may be reacting to your challenges. Dogs are extensions of us, and they are much more sensitive than we realize. They often know us better than we know ourselves.

When training dogs you can become a therapist of all types. You become the owner's friend and confidant. The owners will divulge the jerk that their partner is being or the "issues" their children are having, and even more sinful, like hairstylists, we hear the gossip of who is doing what . . . or who for that matter.

Problems Women Have with Their Canine Companions

The most common problem women have with their dogs is actually the men in their lives. Men often don't think that their dogs need training. Just today I was working with a dog in Palm Beach. The husband who had fought with the wife about getting a private trainer for the German Shepherd puppy said, "There is no problem with this dog. The day I can't train a dog is the day that they bury me."

Dogs listen better to men, so men have an easier time training dogs. It is a proven fact that animals respond better to a man's deep voice. Apparently people do as well. When the Atlanta airport first opened its train system, a woman's voice would come over the loudspeaker. "The doors are now closing. Please step back." There were several injuries because people kept getting caught in the doors. After the airport assessed the situation, the voice was changed to a masculine voice. The injury rate decreased significantly overnight.

Unfortunately, the list doesn't end there. Women's problems are different than men's problems with their dog. The list that follows includes the most common problems we may have with our dogs:

ISSUES
- eating underwear
- nudging and neediness
- crotch sniffing
- aggression
- harassing you during sex—with someone else, of course

Our dog is our baby. Look at those big brown eyes. How can I discipline her? We baby our dogs and give in to their every need and want. We anthropomorphize them, and yet if they don't listen, we rationalize that they are dogs and don't know any better. We simply reason that unlike our children, dogs don't understand. However, dogs do understand. Most people do not give the credit dogs deserve. Dogs are so much smarter than people realize—often smarter than people. Dogs don't understand shades of gray, but they do understand black and white—right and wrong—as long as we show them. It is a proven fact that when you praise a dog's behavior, your dog will repeat the behavior. It has also been proven that when you correct a dog's behavior, your dog will decrease the behavior. However, we have to remember that what we consider a correction is not necessarily a correction in your dog's mind.

Finding Solutions

In this chapter, we will take several approaches for each problem. We will modify the behavior and retrain Samantha, and we'll discuss the management of the problem. Remember: management isn't the long-term solution you want; it is simply a short-term answer. We will also discuss the use of aromatherapy, flower remedies, homeopathy, and naturopathy to help modify behavior and increase the effectiveness of teaching and learning. Finally, we will address the effects of nutrition's role in certain behavior problems.

I am not a veterinarian, nor a homeopathic practitioner of any sort. Any recommendation I make in these areas is strictly from the research and study of experts in these fields and from the application of these practices on my students as well as my own pets. In my lifetime, I have owned a total of sixteen dogs and six cats. They were always my pets until they passed over the Rainbow Bridge. I have also always applied these principles to the dogs I have fostered through rescue. Before you apply any of these techniques, I encourage you to do your own research and only do what is comfortable for you. Remember that your veterinarian has trained extensively and is medically trained, so before you apply any of these remedies, discuss them with her first. I've included a list in the back of this book referring you to practitioners that have training in these particular areas.

Massage therapy, acupressure, and touch are all forms of body work that will help the body heal itself and can help stop the behavior. Not only does it supplement behavior modification training, it also creates a stronger bond for you and Samantha, making you both happier. One particular kind of a massage that has been used successfully on dogs, cats, and horses is the Tellington Touch. It was developed by Linda Tellington-Jones and uses a variety of therapeutic touches to enhance body awareness and release tension that your dog may have, which can create behavior and training problems.

Many times dogs act up because they are frustrated and are in discomfort. They cannot tell us when they are in pain, so they will act out in different ways. I remember one Labrador Retriever that

BACH FLOWER REMEDIES

British physician Edward Bach originally developed flower remedies for humans. These are oral infusions of flowers that act upon and improve the mental, physical, and psychological well-being of humans as well as dogs. They make it easier for the dog to learn while relaxing the dog due to unseen stressors. Two particularly good remedies to start any behavior modification program are chestnut bud and wild oat. These will help open your dog's mind to learning.

You can find flower remedies in any health food store, or if you are in the middle of processed-food land, you can purchase them on the Internet at nelsonbachusa.com. Now to administer them you get to play mad scientist girl.

1. Purchase a one-ounce dropper bottle.
2. Place two drops of the remedy into the bottle.
3. Fill the bottle with one ounce of spring or filtered water creating the solution.
4. Give one to two drops of solution to your dog by mouth two to four times a day, depending on your dog's size.
5. Depending on the intensity of the problem, you will use it anywhere from several days to about two to three weeks.

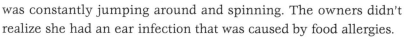

was constantly jumping around and spinning. The owners didn't realize she had an ear infection that was caused by food allergies.

Nutrition has a lot to do with behavior. Think about what may happen to you if you have too much sugar or caffeine. Too many carbohydrates can increase a dog's energy level. A lot of energy can mean excessive chewing, digging, and barking. Too much sodium will make a puppy drink more water, and consequently, the more you put in, the more is put out. Too much protein can increase aggression. It is important that you feed your dog quality food. There is a lot of information out there. It is important that you consult your veterinarian and breeder for the right diet for your dog.

Homeopathy is a form of medicine that was created by a German physician, Dr. Samuel Hahnemann, more than two hundred years ago. It is based on the theory that like cures like. It helps to create balance within the body's systems. Originally developed for humans, it is now successfully used on dogs and is available at your local health food store. One dose will equal one tablet, which also equals five to ten drops or five to ten grains, depending on whether it is in liquid, tablet, or grain form.

Eating Underwear

Eating underwear is a problem that no one ever discusses. Women are too embarrassed to admit it to anyone, and men are too busy watching the football game to notice or care that our favorite underwear is gone and will be found in the yard somewhere the next day.

Why do our dogs participate in such a disgusting habit? We are women, and we give off an odor, and when we ovulate or menstruate, we emit fluids. Dogs, whether we think it is gross or not, like the smell and the taste. Yes, you are red in the face now, but I did warn you that this book would tell it like it is and that if you wanted fluff and political correctness to buy a different book.

It is important to stop this behavior. It can be potentially dangerous. We may joke that we will find it in a land mine in the yard the next day and promptly throw it in the trash, but underwear can create a blockage in your dog, which can lead to surgery. That is certainly not an expense you want to incur nor a stress to which you want to subject your dog.

Behavior Modification

Throw your underwear on the floor and teach Samantha to leave it. This is different from the drop it command. This command actually teaches her not to touch it ever:

1. Throw the underwear on the floor right in front of her face.
2. If she looks at it or even sniffs it, say, "No."
3. Give a tug on the leash if she doesn't respond.

Next move the underwear farther away from her while you move farther away from her. Don't let her think that you are watching her. Remember, she will know that you are setting her up. Thus, you want to set her up so that she doesn't know it. Use mirrors. Find a mirror in your home and walk back and forth in front of it. Look to see what you can see and what you can't see in the mirror. You want a mirror that you can still see when you are in another room. You don't need to see yourself, but you do need to be able to see Samantha. For example, place Samantha in a sit-stay in front of the mirror. She doesn't need to be able to see herself either. It is only important that her reflection is visible to you. Now go into another room and watch her so that she can't see you. Since she cannot see you, she will think that she can grab your panties and get away with it. Watch and wait. If she grabs them, tell her no, return to her, and make her drop them. If she doesn't, correct her and tell her to drop it. At that point, she will drop them. Once she does, give her lots of praise.

Management Solution

Do not leave your underwear on the floor. When you take a shower, make sure you put it right into a hamper with a tight-fitting lid. Your dog will also go into your trash to collect used tampons and napkins. Place the trash can in a cabinet or get one with a tight-fitting lid.

Nudging and Neediness

Nudging can be a big problem for women because when Sam comes up to you, knocks your arm out of the way, and puts her head on your lap, your automatic response is to pet her, thus praising her for what she is doing. Men generally won't respond to nudging with affection. They will tell her to go away.

Neediness is when your dog will not let you out of her sight. This is most commonly seen in sporting and herding breeds. Samantha

FUNNY STORY

Aron, my SchutzHund II German Shepherd whom I bought on one of my trips to Germany, was my pride and joy. One day he was sick, so I took him to Dr. Mike Berkenblit who x-rayed Aron. Dr. B called me and said, "OK, Babette, what did Aron eat?" I had no idea he had eaten anything, but I did break out in a cold sweat thinking that Dr. B would operate and find my underwear inside. Fortunately, Mike found no underwear so I was saved from humiliation, and Aron was fine.

may whine or pace when you leave her alone. She may follow you from room to room and become exceptionally stressed if you are not in her sight. Do not confuse this with a dog that follows you around and lies at your feet. The needy dog will just have to be under your feet touching you and becomes distressed if you go into the bathroom to be left alone.

Behavior Modification

As a woman, you can stop reinforcing the nudging behavior by not petting her each time she asks for it. You can also nudge her right back with your elbow. If she comes back to you, nudge her away again, but don't shove. Have you ever discreetly elbowed your significant other in public when he or she has committed a social faux pas? It is the same thing. You don't want to push her away with your hand because then she thinks that you are praising her. Two or three nudges right back should stop the behavior.

To curb neediness the best thing that you can do is to get Sam used to being alone. If she starts whimpering, whining, or pacing, do not indulge her. Just ignore it.

Management Solution

Massage therapy, aromatherapy, and flower remedies all help soothe your dog's mind. They release tension, and although they don't always completely resolve behavioral issues, they certainly complement the training and behavior modification to create a complete training program.

- **Massage therapy**—Using the Tellington Touch, begin massaging at the hindquarters and move up the body in random sections of her body.
- **Aromatherapy**—When you are massaging her, rub oil of lavender on her. You can also place a drop or two on her ears, which will soothe her.
- **Flower remedy**—A lot of nudging by Sam may mean that she needs to gain more confidence. The use of heather will help to restore her confidence and make her more content. Honeysuckle will help with the separation issue.

Crotch Sniffing

Do you ever have your girlfriends come over and Samantha goes straight for their crotch and begins sniffing? This is where most of women's pheromones are emitted, which tells your dog a lot about your friends. Are they nice? Afraid? One sniff will tell her all she needs to know. Dogs who may not normally sniff the crotch may decide to when a woman is menstruating.

Behavior Modification

There are several ways to correct crotch sniffing. Heel Samantha to the front door when you greet guests. Put her into a sit-stay, or even better, a down-stay. She is less likely to get up from a down-stay than a sit-stay. Make her stay until you open the door for your guest. Once your friend comes in, release Samantha. If she beelines for the crotch, say, "No, leave it." As soon as she stops, give her lots of praise.

Management Solution

When a dog is using her nose often, it means her body is in balance, which is of course a good thing. Yet, you want to curb that crotch sniffing. You want her to be healthy, and treating her homeopathically and balancing her nutritional needs will make her healthier and easier to teach.

- **Homeopathy**—Give Samantha one dose a day of phosphorus 30C for five to seven days. The phosphorus will enhance Samantha's scenting ability, which will allow her to learn about your friends without being overly obnoxious.
- **Nutrition**—Make sure that Samantha is receiving enough vitamin B—this will keep her calm. If she is not receiving enough, she will be more prone to a higher activity level. Chelated magnesium is another important mineral she should be receiving. If Samantha weighs less than fifteen pounds, one hundred mg would be a good daily dose. For dogs weighing between fifteen and fifty pounds, give three hundred mg, and for dogs weighing more than fifty pounds, give six hundred mg. Saint-John's-wort, which is what we women take to calm our nerves during times of stress, will also help calm Samantha.

Aggression

Aggression can be a very difficult problem for women. There are several reasons why it is more common with women dog owners. I emphasize and use the words *more common* very loosely. There are several variables: men won't allow a dog to get nasty, unless they really want a mean dog. If they do, then it is not a problem. Women, on the other hand, will condone the behavior. They get a dog for protection, and they don't stop the signs of aggression. They like it because the dog is "protecting them." If a dog bites them, women are more apt to blame themselves while a man is more likely to smack the dog—not that I agree with it—and throw the dog outside.

Some women who are in abusive relationships will also allow a dog to be aggressive, either toward them or others. They allow this behavior for several reasons: (1) They are afraid to stop the dog's aggression toward them; after all if they allow themselves to be mistreated by a partner, they will certainly allow it from a dog. (2) If the dog is aggressive toward others but not to them, they may feel that the dog will protect them and stop anything "really bad" from happening. (3) They are unable to tell an abusive partner that they are not comfortable with the dog nor want to have such an aggressive dog. (4) The dog may be their only friend.

Behavior Modification

There are many things that can be done to combat and control aggression. Allowing for population growth, the actual percentage of the dog population of truly aggressive dogs has greatly decreased over the last forty years. If you have an aggressive dog, you need to get professional help immediately. This is definitely not the time to get a bargain when it comes to training your aggressive dog. You want to hire the best trainer you can find. There will be more on how to find a professional in Chapter 15. Hire several to come out and do an evaluation for you so that they can see the dynamics of your dog's home. Don't hesitate to pay for a consultation. Be wary of free evaluations.

Most busy competent trainers don't have the time for a free evaluation. Anyone who doesn't charge for his or her "evaluation" will not necessarily be telling you the truth. They are there to "sell" you

CASE IN POINT

I spent the summer of 1994 with my dad in Los Angeles. We went to do an aggression consultation with a Chow Chow. The quiet, timid owner lived with the dog and her boyfriend and seemed so afraid of this dog. As we took a history of the dog, I noticed a very light bruising around the owner's eye. After the session I told my dad that I thought the boyfriend was abusing her. He hadn't noticed the very light black eye. He asked why and I told him that it was just a gut feeling based on a few things: (1) the girl had the bruise; (2) she was afraid of the dog; and (3) the boyfriend didn't seem to care that she was afraid. Although my dad told them that they had a serious problem, the boyfriend wanted to keep the dog even though he had bitten his girlfriend and she didn't want the dog living in the house.

About a month later, my dad called me on the telephone. I was right. The boyfriend had been beating up the woman. The dog was continually showing aggression and the boyfriend was doing nothing to stop the behavior. He was keeping the dog and was very happy with his decision. The dog probably had aggressive tendencies to begin with, and his behavior only became worse because the woman allowed the dog to behave so. The abuser—the man in this case—didn't do anything to curtail the dog's aggressive behavior. The woman was not in a position to stop the aggression herself.

a training job. The evaluation should include a history of the dog, including all bites and involved factors, and the trainers putting their hands on the dog and working with her. If the trainer is sitting down with you and discussing the issues and theory, he or she is not solving the problem. If after one consultation you haven't been taught better leash handling skills and the trainer hasn't worked and improved your dog, find one who will. You will pay good money for an honest evaluation. The trainer is walking into a home with an unknown dog of aggressive nature. Just like police officers, the trainers are putting themselves on the line. One good bite could put a trainer out of work for a long time, if not forever.

Some dog owners choose to work with a behaviorist and medication. Like all good trainers the behaviorist will want a physical exam for the dog including a complete blood screening and a serum chemistry panel. Additional tests may be ordered based on the results of the blood and serum tests. I recommend these tests before working with medication so you'll know exactly where the results are coming from.

Many owners will call me and say they want group classes for their dog because their dog is not good with other dogs or people. They figure if they got the dog around other dogs and people, the dog would be better. Although in theory that is sound logic, in practical application it is not a good idea. In my experience I have found that in the beginning it is better to work with the dog and owner privately. This gives you the opportunity to work with your dog and improve your handling skills in a much less distracting, thus less stressful environment. You will receive the one-on-one attention that is needed in aggression solutions.

Management Solution

I can't emphasize it enough: if you are dealing with an issue, especially aggression, it is imperative that you confront and solve the problem using all the tools available to you; this includes nutrition, massage therapy, aromatherapy, flower remedies, and homeopathy.

- **Nutrition**—I suggest that you switch your dog to a lower protein diet and decrease the raw meat content. Examine the ingredients on the bag. Stay away from corn. This carbohydrate is going to increase your dog's energy. Very energetic, aggressive dogs are not a good combination. An increase in niacin, which can be found in liver, lean meat, wheat germ, and eggs, will help in curbing aggression as well as many behavioral disorders. Incidentally, niacin has also been shown to be helpful in decreasing seizures. Consult your veterinarian.
- **Massage therapy**—Using the Tellington Touch method, take your index, middle, and ring fingers and randomly place them on Samantha's head. Move around in a complete circle. Each circle should last less than one second. Move around her head, ears, and mouth. Massage her neck and along her spine. Move around the rest of her body down to her tail. Do this each day beginning with five-minute sessions. Lengthen the amount of time. A very hard and aggressive dog may give you a hard time at first, so start slowly and work for a very short period of time. If you are consistent with this you will

find that your dog will relax. Aggressive dogs are very keyed up and will always be tense. They need to relax.

- **Aromatherapy**—Essential oil of bergamot will help tame an aggressive dog. You can place two to four drops on her collar—depending on her size. The scent will last up to six hours. Use it once a day.
- **Flower remedies**—Oregon grape and tiger lily can be used in combination with your aggressive dog. Using these two in combination will help decrease activity, hostility, and "unprovoked attacks out of nowhere," as well as encourage cooperation. Bach's remedy of vine will help curtail bossy attitudes, which will increase into aggression. Beech is also good for treating aggressive dogs.
- **Homeopathy**—The following homeopaths can be used to treat aggression in your dog by adding five to ten drops to a tablespoon of water once a day. As her condition and attitude improve, use them less frequently until the problem is solved:

    If Samantha gives a warning before attack, then Hyoscyamus will work well.

    If Samantha is the kind of girl that attacks at any given moment when people either enter your home or when they leave, then Nux Vomica is a great homeopath.

    Chamomilla 200x is beneficial when you have an ongoing battle with Samantha. If she is constantly fighting you for the alpha position, Chamomilla will help calm her attitude.

When Samantha Is a Peeping Tom

Sex, sex, and more sex. Sex sells and it is because everyone enjoys it: your dog, your partner, your neighbor, and even your parents. Oh, no—it is a gross thought. Well, what do you do when your canine wants a threesome? This is another problem that no one ever discusses. What's a woman to do when her dog starts whining and crying and trying to jump up on the bed while she is doing the deed? You can lock her out of the room, but it is pretty difficult to concentrate and fake orgasms if the dog's at the door scratching to get inside. That can be very frustrating for you and your partner.

Behavior Modification

Doing your obedience exercises will help. You want Samantha to learn to stay by herself. So when you aren't doing the deed, practice locking her out of the room. Practice keeping her in her crate. You can place her in there with a favorite toy when you are having your fun. If she has a bed in your room, put her in a down-stay (this is one reason practicing down-stays with distractions is important!). If she is persistent, you will need a patient partner. Each time she starts scratching at the door, jump up, swing open the door, tell her no, and close the door. You will have to be more persistent than she, but in no time at all you will no longer wonder who is grunting— your dog or your partner.

Management Solutions

Be like a man when it comes to sex; keep trying all solutions until she relents. After all, you will both still respect each other in the morning. But most importantly, remember one thing: "love me, love my dog."

- **Flower remedy**—Rescue remedy has a general calming effect and will help subdue your dog.
- **Aromatherapy**—Massaging her ears with lavender will also relax her, and she will be more likely to lie down and go to sleep.
- **Crate**—Tell her to go to her kennel. Give her a yummy bone to chew and keep her in there until the deed is done.

Help!
I Need Somebody!
Not Just Anybody!

If you want the best man for the job,

hire a woman.

—Anonymous

Unlike men, women aren't afraid to ask for directions. We realize that sometimes a professional is needed. Sometimes we all need extra direction, motivation, and an education. We hire personal trainers to motivate us to work out. We hire mechanics to fix our cars because they know what they are doing.

Although you have read this and several other books—all of which contradict one another—you feel that you just need to get some individual help. Yet, your neighbor told you that a group class is better than private instruction. Now that you are completely confused the only thing you know for sure is that you need to do something more. I have trained dogs in all settings—group lessons, private lessons, day school, in-home tutoring, boarding school, and doggy day care, and all of these programs are good.

There are pros and cons to each, and I think it is important to truly understand them so that you can evaluate fairly which alternative is best for your specific needs and goals.

Group Lessons

Group lessons tend to be the least expensive. You don't necessarily get one-on-one attention, but you do get the benefit of interacting with other dog owners and dogs. Depending on the individual instructor, there may be structured playtime for the dogs. Some schools feel that if you want your dog to play, you should bring her to a dog park. One trainer says, "Why should they pay me for playtime? I am there to train the dog." Courses will vary in content and curriculum. Some schools will offer in six weeks what others may teach in six months.

Q&A

Are group classes really better for my dog?

Yes and no. Quality group classes are good for every dog so that they learn how to behave around other dogs and distractions. The downside is that if you have a difficult dog or need extra help, you will not receive the special attention and training that you and your dog desperately need.

My dog is mean to other dogs, so one of my friends said I should do group lessons. Should I sign my dog up?

In my opinion, unless you have both received intensive private lessons with a degree of success, it is not wise to take a group class if your dog is aggressive. If you and your dog have had previous training, group classes are a good idea because she will not be there to learn new things, as much as you are there to get her used to other dogs in a structured environment. Understand, however, that for liability reasons the instructor may make another recommendation.

Private Lessons

This type of training is usually done in the home. However, many schools offer training for a lower price when you go to their facility. There are a couple of reasons for this: (1) you decrease the trainer's travel time so they don't need to charge you as much as an in-home trainer would charge. You are the one who gets to drive in the snow, rain, and fog; and (2) they also tend to have a higher overhead than an in-home trainer so the school will need a higher volume of students, which means they have to have competitive prices so they don't lose their clients to cheaper alternatives.

A great benefit of private lessons is that both your dog and you will receive a one-on-one education. Private lessons enable you to inform the trainer what type of lifestyle you have, what kinds of challenges you have, and what type of relationship and home life you have with your dog. A good trainer will know how to approach each dog differently and how to train the dog based on the dog's unique personality and the owner's particular lifestyle. It is difficult to use a cookie-cutter approach for all breeds. You will then find certain breeds are more difficult than others, but I don't train dogs like that. I treat them like an individual, and quite honestly, the dogs are easy. Typically, it is usually the owners who are most difficult to train. In fact, training the owner is 80 percent of what we do. We have to convince owners to think outside the box and adapt their communication skills to their dogs. It is a lot easier to train a dog than an owner. The trainer needs to understand the dynamics of the family. I have met owners over the years who weren't happy with the last trainer they had. Often the former trainer wasn't bad, but he or she made the mistake of trying to change the household dynamics or influencing the owner into

LITTLE-KNOWN FACT

Many people will tell you that your dog needs to socialize. While true, many don't realize that most of the socialization has already taken place. Your dog has learned how to play with other dogs during her first eight weeks with her littermates.

Nevertheless, socialization is important. You can simultaneously train and socialize your dog. Practice training your dog at the beach or the dog park. Allow your dog play breaks with other dogs you meet. Go to your local Starbucks and practice sit-stays and down-stays while you enjoy a cup of cappuccino. It is so very European. Besides, you never know who you might meet. Remember dogs are mate magnets.

creating a utopian household for the dog. Although animal lovers very often have very strong opinions on the way people should treat their dogs, they don't see that some things just aren't realistic for the average family. As a mom, single woman, or an empty nester, you want your dog to behave, not jump on children, not chew the sofa, and not drag you down the street. Good personal trainers will recognize that you need to develop a dynamic relationship with your dog and incorporate your dog into your home, not the other way around.

CASE IN POINT

I remember one very nice lady who lived in the cutest cottage in Palm Beach. She was a single mom who had adopted a mixed breed and was very frustrated. The dog was destroying the nine-hundred-square-foot home. The home was already in disrepair. The woman had fallen on very hard times and the dog was the only hope for happiness she and her daughter had at the time. She had hired a trainer to help with all of the problems. The trainer made suggestions, such as send the dog to day care, put a dog run in the back yard, and walk her three miles a day. These options were just not realistic. Although these things could have helped manage the dog's chewing and destructiveness, they were not realistic for the owner. The trainer said that unless the owner did everything she told her she wouldn't work with her. The woman simply couldn't afford day care for the dog. The town of Palm Beach would never allow a dog run in the yard and walking the dog three miles a day would be a real time challenge for her.

A good trainer would've made suggestions that were in line with her finances and daily routine.

With private lessons, you will pay more money than in a group, but you will get more for your money. For example, let's say you pay $150 for six weeks of group classes, one hour each week with eight other students. That's a total of 360 minutes with the instructor shared with eight other students. To say that in the best-case scenario you will have 40 minutes of the instructor's undivided attention is a stretch. However, if you take one 60-minute session with an instructor privately, you already have had more one-on-one attention than in a six-week group class.

Q&A

Are private lessons worth it?

Yes. In my experience and from the experiences of my mentors, there is no doubt that private lessons offer better quality training for both you and your dog. I tell everyone—if it is in the budget, then do it. If you cannot afford it, then do at least the group class.

CASE IN POINT

I don't remember Lara originally calling me, but I certainly remember the following call: "Hi, I called you about a year ago. I need help with my dog, Sabrina. I am still having trouble with her. I had told you that I couldn't afford the private lessons. You suggested that at the very least I should go to a group class. I found the cheapest group class around and it got me through the first year. I have been saving my money because I know that Sabrina needs you. Can you still help us?" This was the perfect advice for a young single girl who was just out of school. She confided that if I hadn't told her to take a group class, even if it wasn't the best quality, she would have had to get rid of Sabrina because she just couldn't manage her anymore.

Today Lara is one of my best friends, and Sabrina is a great dog. It would have broken Lara's heart to find a new home for Sabrina—the little mixed breed that someone gave her while in law school. Sabrina today weighs close to ninety pounds, and Lara still stays that the best thing she did was the group class and later, after she saved her money, the private lessons.

At what age, should I start the training?

This question receives so much misinformation that I become very frustrated and disappointed. The wrong advice on this question has led many dogs to the pound. No dog is ever too young or too old to learn. I always tell people to start training the minute the dog walks into their

BAD ADVICE

About eight years ago a pet shop owner called me asking if I knew a certain "behaviorist." I told her I did. The owner told me she had sold a Miniature Pinscher to a couple about seven months prior. They were working with the "behaviorist" for a house-training issue. The "behaviorist" told them that before they could house-train the dog, they needed to establish themselves as pack leader. They started the house-training after working on obedience for several months, as per the "expert's" advice. After the dog failed to house-train, the "expert" deemed the dog "genetically defective" and "impossible to house-train." The owners wanted their money back and to get rid of the dog.

Miniature Pinschers are difficult dogs to house-train. This "expert" had allowed the dog to develop bad habits for several months before addressing the house-training issue, which in my opinion should have been addressed in the very first lesson. During the first lesson, they may not have had a "problem," but the "behaviorist" should have recognized if a potential problem existed and that part of her responsibility was making sure that the owners were doing what they needed to succeed. Please don't wait to train your dog. Do what my friend Lara did. My mantra is "Do something. Something is better than nothing. Do anything. Anything is better than setting your dog up to fail."

home. This way you stop problems from developing and start your dog out on the right paw.

Day School

Day school is not a new concept, but it isn't that popular yet either. People can drop off their dogs in the morning and pick them up at the end of the day. The dogs are trained in an outstanding, real-life environment. I had the treat of spending a few days with Sandy and Carlos Mejias, the owners of the Olde Towne School for Dogs in Alexandria, Virginia. They started the first day school for dogs in 1975. The school is a trainer's dream.

Day school allows dogs to learn in the presence of other dogs while getting one-on-one attention. The trainers will go out in packs together walking through town with their students. At the end of each day, the owner spends a few minutes learning what Missy learned that day. Although the owner is learning along with the dog, the owner is not placed with as much responsibility of practicing each day as she is expected to in private or group lessons.

Q&A

Don't I need to see what my dog is learning?

Any good school is going to show you upon gradation how to work your dog. Would you rather build your own car and learn how to drive it or have a professional build it and teach you how to drive it? It is the same thing.

I am afraid that the trainer may not be nice to my dog if I am not around.

You will know if there is a problem. If you go to a trainer with a proven track record, you should not be concerned. The stories of abusive dog

WHO TRAINED WHO?

I remember a seven-year-old English Springer Spaniel named Senator. Senator's owner, Jeff, came to us for day school training with his dog. The dog had never been asked to do anything, so you can imagine that Senator needed some boot camp. He had never been disciplined for anything and to say that the dog was a hellion is an understatement. Each morning Senator would come pulling in on the leash and Jeff would be laughing the entire time running to keep up. Several sessions later, Jeff's girlfriend said to me, "Senator is so much better. I realize Jeff will allow him to revert back but if he doesn't revert back all the way, it will have been worth it." About five years later, a friend of Jeff's called to register for classes. He let us know that Senator was still a wild man but nothing like he was before the training with us. Like anything, you get what you put into it.

trainers are tales that are very few and very far between. If you don't feel comfortable with the trainer, participate in a different type of training.

In-Home Tutoring

In-home tutoring is something very similar to the day school. This type of training entails having the trainer go to your home on a daily basis and work your dog for you. As with the day school concept, you don't have to be there. It is very labor-intensive for the trainer, but the results are outstanding if you keep up with this type of training.

We do in-home tutoring quite a bit in Palm Beach. Many people only come down for the winter and have very busy social calendars. They like the fact that they are getting high-quality training without having to send the dog away. The dog gets picked up and returned an hour or so later to the home after an intensive training session in the park or walking through town. The trainer will also train your dog in your home or yard. You will notice that your dog will love the sound of the trainer ringing the doorbell. There will be a difference in your dog overnight, and you can learn along with your dog without having to take her to school for the whole day.

Boarding School

For dogs like Senator boarding school is a great option. It is wonderful if you are going to go on vacation; you can kill two birds with one stone, so to speak. Maybe you are having some work done in your home. This option is very good, but you must make an attitude change when Missy comes home. It is important that you work with the trainer to learn Missy's commands and your new rules. To continue training you may want to do some private or group classes with the trainer to maintain the new program. If you do not follow the new rules when Missy comes home, you will have wasted your money.

MORE BAD ADVICE

When Carrie called to cancel her appointment for her Tibetan Terrier, she told me that a breeder at the dog show told her not to train right now because Oreo was teething. The rationale was that because the dog was losing her baby teeth, she would associate training with the negative.

This was the most ridiculous thing I ever heard! When your children are losing their teeth, do you allow them to talk back and misbehave and not teach them right from wrong just because they have their adult teeth coming in? Of course you don't.

Doggy Day Care

Doggy day care is a popular concept for helping active or lonely dogs. This is a fun way to allow your dog to vent some of her energy. There are day cares and there are day cares. When Siobhan sent King, a Rottweiler, to day care, she found that at home he became more stubborn and more dominating. She didn't want that behavior encouraged. After examining the situation, she realized that at this particular day care, there wasn't any structure and the dogs were permitted to do what they wanted, when they wanted, and if that included dogs picking on other dogs, they allowed it. Once Siobhan switched day cares, she found that the new one wouldn't allow unruly play. The second day care understood the difference between constructive play and destructive play, and King is still a student there.

I have had folks over the years tell me that they would rather pay the money for day care than spend it on training. Yes, your dog will be better behaved after a fun day at camp because she's tired from all the playing and running around, but you are giving a short-term Band-Aid to something for which training will give a permanent solution. There is nothing wrong with day care. However, if your dog has problems that need to be solved, you will get dollar for dollar a better value with a program that focuses on training.

I do encourage you to send your dog to day care at least a couple of times a week if you can't exercise her regularly or you work long hours. Just remember that day care is not a substitute for good training.

A Quick Word on Exercise

It is obvious that a lot of exercise will help wear out your active hound, but many times your dog will then increase her endurance, thus requiring more exercise. Be cautious of the amount of exercise and the type of exercise you give her. Many times, a hard game of retrieving is more productive than a five-mile run. I recommend retrieve games with a bouncy, unpredictable toy such as a Kong toy because when you throw it, your dog never knows where it is going to bounce. She has to work twice as hard to catch it and bring it back and won't get bored with the game. Retrieving games build her muscles and agility. Running can be hard on joints. Swimming is great exercise and very good for the hips.

Questions to Ask a Potential Trainer

In large cities, trainers can be a dime a dozen. In small towns, there may be just one. Now that I have given you the options, let's discuss the questions you can ask a potential trainer. I will also give you a trainer's interpretation of the question and his or her possible answer. This will teach you to read through the lines.

First, let's talk about how to read the ads that you will see. Some common ads will say "training for twenty years"; "veterinarian recommended"; or "positive training only." This year I opened my yellow pages to see my new advertisement. I was amazed at all of the new dog trainers in town and how they claimed so many years of experience, yet I hadn't seen their ads before. That is not to say that they didn't move from elsewhere, but I want to tell you about one man who called me.

He asked about my programs and then said, "You sound very young." I do have a young voice. I said that if I told him about my experience, he probably, understandably, wouldn't believe me. I began to tell him how I worked in my dad's kennel from 1974 during the weekends and in the summer. I explained that I did have more experience than most others due to my dad's reputation; his very large school at one time employed more than one hundred people training and caring for dogs. I then told him that in 1989 I began training full-time on my own. He explained that he realized after talking to a couple of trainers that they would say they had twenty years training dogs, but they worked at other jobs during the day. He didn't feel they should say they had "twenty years' experience." So he hired me to train his dog. Determine what twenty years' experience means. Is it part-time, on and off, between jobs? Also beware of trainers who attribute their training experience to training their own dog.

Trainers who write misleading advertisements are not necessarily going to reveal the truth to you when asked. Ask if you can observe a class in action. Over the years I have had people ask me for references. I laugh and think to myself, do they actually think I am going to give them the name of someone who will say something bad about us? I remember one trainer who was just starting out. She gave the people the name and number of her best friend, aunt, and grandmother. There is nothing wrong with asking for a reference, but remember that you could be getting anyone on the phone. When people ask us for references, we tell them to open up the yellow pages and call half a dozen veterinarians and ask them what they have heard about us. That way they can choose whom to ask and get the most honest opinion possible. I have many clients who would love to vouch for me, but I personally don't like giving out their numbers and allowing their privacy to be invaded. I don't like receiving calls during my dinner, and I'm sure my loyal clients don't either.

Check the trainer's experience. Ask around town. Call the local humane society to see if any complaints have been filed. Instead of checking for-profit business bureaus, you are better off contacting

TRUE STORY

I had a woman who called me who had a very aggressive Great Dane. The dog was fully grown and had bitten a few people. The woman was living temporarily with a boyfriend and the dog bit him as well. Because of the dog's history and the cause of the bite, she called me trying to decide if she could fix the dog or if she should euthanize the dog. After talking with her, I decided that for everyone's safety, I needed to be accompanied by an assistant. I gave her a quote for an evaluation. She mentioned that someone else was coming for free. I explained to her why I was charging my fee. Basically it is due to the risk that I (and all dog trainers) put myself in when dealing with an aggressive dog. For instance, I could get injured and be out of work for a while. I told her I would give her a fair assessment and that after I worked with her and the dog we could discuss the pros and cons of each option. Those options were keeping and training the dog, keeping the dog and hoping the problem would go away without training, placing the dog in another home and the options for doing that, or euthanizing the dog. She wanted to think about it. She called me back and said, "Could you please come? I really need to figure out what to do." Deeming this an emergency because of the emotional involvement, we squeezed her in the next day.

After taking a case history, we all went outside with the dog. Because of his size and for our safety, my husband and I worked him together. We then taught the owner a few things so that she had a better understanding not only of her dog, but also, and more importantly, of how she could manage his behavior until she decided what she wanted to do with him. We gave her our evaluation and our prognosis. She decided that euthanasia was the choice she was going to make. She tearfully wrote the check and told us how the "trainer" who gave the "free evaluation" didn't even take the dog out of the crate. He never put his hands on the dog or worked the dog. He just told her that her dog could be trained and the charges. She thanked us again as we left. It was very sad and about a week later she called to give us a report. It is hard to call owners who are in that position for a follow-up. You don't know if you are going make them more upset by calling. She had let him go peacefully. She knew she had done the right thing because she saw how he was with us, and she knew that he was happier for it.

If you have difficult problems and the first trainer wants to give you a free evaluation, there is nothing wrong with taking it, but don't discard the trainer who will charge you for her time and knowledge to give you an honest, forthright opinion.

Abraham Lincoln once said, "A lawyer's time and knowledge is his stock-in-trade." Captain Haggerty said, "So is a dog trainer's."

your local courthouse and checking to see if anyone has sued the company or trainer. If the company or trainer had had many lawsuits in a short period of time, take that as a warning sign. If you are very unsure, ask to do a private lesson so that you can feel out the trainer and make sure you are comfortable with the trainer, the techniques, and the results. Any good trainer will show you improvement after the first lesson. Be cautious of "free evaluations." Very often, they are sales pitches. Any good trainer who understands and

SAD STORY WITH A HAPPY ENDING

Bob Maida is an excellent trainer in northern Virginia who has taught me quite a bit and has been a longtime friend of my dad's and mine. Anyway, Bob called me up one day to let me know he's started training a people-aggressive Doberman. The owners had previously used a trainer who believed in totally positive reinforcement with no corrections. This trainer also insisted they buy the book he had written, which was about a completely different breed of dog—a breed, I might add, that is known more for its outgoing, kid-proof personality than for aggression problems. The owners wanted to help their dog, and after three lessons of the trainer sitting with them on the couch and not working with them or the dog, they asked to stop the training. Long story short, the trainer didn't return their phone calls or their E-mails. He decided that he was going to keep all of their money. Fortunately for this dog, the owners didn't get rid of him, which is what most people would have done in this situa-

tion. They loved their dog so they hired Bob. During the first lesson, Bob had the dog out with other dogs. The dog was better—he was no longer lunging and the owners were ecstatic. Some more work needed to be done with the dog, but for the first time, they had hope.

Consequently, the owners sued and won the case against the trainer who chose to sit and talk with them instead of solving the problem proactively. If you don't see results and improvement in your dog after the first lesson, evaluate whether you have chosen the program that best fits your needs. "Trainers" like the one who was sued do an injustice to the dog-training profession, and ultimately dogs end up in the pound and are killed because their owners feel that the dogs are hopeless, when that is not the case. The discussion of learning theory is very thought-provoking and stimulating, but how are you going to stop problems just by talking or choosing to ignore them altogether?

has trained many dogs knows the right questions to ask you and can make a recommendation over the phone. A good trainer doesn't need to see your house or car to give you a price.

Most busy, competent trainers don't have the time for a free evaluation. Anyone who doesn't charge for his or her "evaluation" will not necessarily be telling you the truth. They are there to "sell" you a training job. You will pay good money for an honest evaluation.

The evaluation should include a history of the dog, including all medical and behavioral issues, and the trainer's putting his or her hands on the dog and working the dog. If the trainer is merely sitting down with you and discussing the issues and theory, he or she is not solving the problem. If after one consultation you haven't been taught better handling skills for controlling your dog or the trainer hasn't worked and improved your dog, find one who will.

A woman once called me who had a seven-year-old German Shepherd Dog that had bitten her son's ten-year-old friend in the face, breaking skin. The bite occurred six months before her call. She wanted to know if I could "fix" the dog. She was unwilling to pay a consultation fee. She told me I should do it for free because she was now being sued. She didn't care enough to stop the bite from occurring nor to "fix" the dog when the bite originally happened. Yet, she wanted me to travel on my time to her multimillion dollar home to see her dog and tell her if I could "fix" the dog for "not a lot of money." This woman had more problems than just an aggressive dog. We gladly sent her on her way. When one is too consumed with oneself, it is difficult to see the real problem.

Methods

Ask about methods. This can be tricky, unless you understand the ins and outs of different methods

POP QUIZ

Your two-year-old child is running to the street. Would you

A. call him to you?

B. ignore the behavior, hoping that will extinguish it?

C. offer him a cookie?

D. grab him and stop him from running into the street?

I don't know about you, but I picked *D*. My son doesn't always come when called, especially when something across the street is more appealing. If I ignore his behavior, he will keep going and I can watch him get—oh, my God—get hit by a car. If I can get his attention and offer him a cookie, it would only reinforce his running into the street. Yes, directing him back toward the sidewalk and telling him that it is dangerous and intolerable to run into the street will make him think twice. A simple squint of the eyes, a deep voice, and a firm look are all he needs.

and techniques. A buzzword lately is *positive reinforcement*. In my experience, all trainers use "positive reinforcement." It has become politically incorrect in very small yet very vociferous circles to ever tell a dog no or to use any type of correction. But how can you solve problems when the dog is only rewarded for doing well? You didn't call a trainer because your dog is good all the time. You called because she is doing naughty things. But ultimately, you need to do what feels most comfortable to you.

Child Rearing and Dog Training

They are very similar. There is a great book titled *Dog Trainer's Guide to Parenting*, which has terrific application to dog training. Over the years I have had many owners who were also parents say, "Babette, you are going to be a great mom if you're the same way with your children as you are with my dog. Your kids will have it made." Quite the compliment. I just didn't realize at the time how similar kid training and dog training were.

One day I was at church with my son; he went running over to an electrical socket. I sternly said, "No" with small, determined eyes and took his hand away from the socket. He looked at me quizzically as my response was not something he was used to seeing. He then went to touch it again, this time quite cautiously while watching me. I repeated myself a bit more sharply and pulled his little hand away more firmly. He was getting the idea. He was more curious at my response, and, with a smile on my face, I told him he was a good boy. Again, he watched me and slowly moved his hand toward the socket, I said, "No" and shook my head. He immediately stopped and smiled. I smiled back, gave him a hug and kiss, and told him he was a great kid. Every now and then, if we are somewhere and he points to an uncovered socket, he looks at me first and says, "Oh, look." I shake my head, and he smiles and walks away from it. He now understands that if he doesn't go near it, he gets praise.

Some Final Suggestions

When you are looking to hire a dog trainer, a great resource is professional organizations, such as the International Association of Canine Professionals, which requires that members demonstrate proof of at least five years of full-time training experience. Members must also be sponsored by two other professionals. The National Association of Dog Obedience Instructors (NADOI) was originally developed for those who competed in obedience competition, but it has since welcomed those who train professionally but not necessarily for competition. In order to become endorsed by NADOI, you must fill out a rigorous questionnaire explaining your experience, techniques, and education. It is a laborious process and the requirements are very stringent. The Association of Pet Dog Trainers (APDT) was founded in 1993. The APDT's mission is to promote and educate trainers and owners on "dog-friendly" techniques. It has an open membership policy and also provides voluntary certification testing.

Examine your goals and desires. List what is important to you. For example, the last time I bought a car I wrote down a list of what I wanted. I wanted a certain kind of car, a certain color, and specific options. My husband and I then went to find who was going to fulfill my needs at the price we wanted to pay. I suggest you do the same when choosing a dog trainer. Decide your priorities—price, convenience, goals, quality, and experience of trainer. Shop around, call local veterinarians, observe classes, and examine the curriculum. Remember that it is quite often like comparing apples to oranges, so attempt to draw the parallels so that you can make a prudent decision.

No matter what route you choose, what you put into it, you will get out of it. Be sure to consider your goals for training and investigate. Remember: no two trainers are alike, and the results will also be based on what you put into the training and whether you practice the techniques with your dog. Don't fail your dog, and she won't fail you.

Final Treat

God sat down for a moment when the
dog was finished to observe what He
had created. He knew that it was good,
that nothing was lacking and that He
could not have done better.

—Rainer Maria Rilke

How lucky we are to be women! We can cook, clean, raise children, have careers, be supportive of our significant others, and still remember to feed the dog. The secret we have kept from men for so long is that dogs are truly woman's best friend. The secret is now out. With women's liberation and feminism entrenched in our society, it was just a matter of time. Anita Loos is quoted as saying, "I'm furious about the women's liberationists. They keep getting up on soapboxes and proclaiming that women are brighter than men. That's true, but it should be kept very quiet or it ruins the whole racket." It may very well ruin everything, but people everywhere now know that dogs were never *man's* best friend.

I am glad that I have been able to help your dog become your best friend. You have now begun a long and wonderful life with your dog. I thank you for giving your dog the opportunity to become your best friend. You will never be sorry that you gave your heart to your dog. Your dog will thank you a million times over in uncompromising love and devotion—a quality you will only find in a dog.

At this point you can now start tricks, agility, or any other training. Remember that your dog is a lot smarter than you realize. Watch and pay attention; I promise you that she is not the lemon brain some will have you believe.

If you do have questions, please feel free to personally contact me. I will be more than happy to help you in any way possible or refer you to a competent, results-producing trainer in your area. I ask one thing of you: whatever you do, don't ever give up on your dog because she will never give up on you.

Enjoy!

Happy Training!

Proud graduate Cali Nicklaus. Photo by Babette Haggerty-Brennan.

Gonzo Brown waves good-bye. Photo by Babette Haggerty-Brennan.

Resources and Recommended Reading

BOOKS

Arden, Darlene. *The Angell Memorial Animal Hospital Book of Wellness and Preventive Care for Dogs*. Chicago: Contemporary Books, 2002.

Benjamin, Carol Lea. *Surviving Your Dog's Adolescence: A Positive Training Program*. New York: John Wiley & Sons, 1993.

Coren, Stanley. *Why We Love the Dogs We Do*. New York: Fireside, 2000.

Diller, Steven. *Dogs and Their People*. New York: Hyperion, 1998.

Evans, Job Michael. *People, Pooches and Problems: Understanding, Controlling, and Correcting Problem Behavior in Your Dog*. New York: John Wiley & Sons, 2001.

Frost, April. *Beyond Obedience: Training with Awareness for You and Your Dog*. New York: Harmony Books, 1998.

Gavrielle-Gold, Joel. *When Pets Come Between Partners: How to Keep Love—and Romance—in the Human/Animal Kingdom of Your Home*. New York: John Wiley & Sons, 2000.

Graham, Helen, and Gregory Vlamis. *Bach Flower Remedies for Animals*. Moray, Scotland: Findhorn Press, Inc., 1999.

Haggerty, Captain Arthur J. *How to Teach Your Dog to Talk*. New York: Fireside, 2000.

—— . *How to Get Your Pet into Show Business*. New York: Hungry Minds, Inc., 1994.

—— . *Zen and the Art of Dog Training* (to be released in 2004).

Haggerty, Captain Arthur J., and Carol Lea Benjamin. *Dog Tricks*. New York: Black Dog and Leventhal Publishing, 1996.

Hansen, Harold. *The Dog Trainer's Guide to Parenting: Rewarding Good Behavior, Practicing Patience and Other Positive Techniques That Work*. Naperville, Ill.: Sourcebooks Trade, 2000.

Pitcairn, Richard H., and Susan Hubble Pitcairn. *Dr. Pitcairn's Complete Guide to Natural Health for Dogs and Cats*. Emmaus, Pa.: Rodale Press, 1995.

Siegal, Mordecai, and Matthew Margolis. *Good Dog, Bad Dog: Dog Training Made Easy*. New York: Henry Holt & Company, Inc., 1991.

VIDEOS

The following videos may be purchased online at HaggertyDog.com:

"Dog Training for Women" by Babette Haggerty-Brennan.

"Dog Tricks with Captain Haggerty" by Captain Haggerty.

"Preventing Dog Problems" by Captain Haggerty.

"Zen and the Art of Dog Training" by Captain Haggerty and Babette Haggerty-Brennan.

HELPFUL WEBSITES

AltVetMed
www.altvetmed.com

America Academy of Veterinary Medical Acupuncture
www.aavma.com

American Holistic Veterinary Medical Association
www.ahvma.org

American Kennel Club
www.akc.org

American Veterinary Medical Association (AVMA)
www.avma.org

Aromatherapy for Animals
www.aromanotes.com/animals

Babette Haggerty-Brennan
www.BabetteHaggerty-Brennan.com

Dog Training for Women
www.dogtrainingforwomen.com

Dr. Ian Billinghurst (pioneer in raw food for dogs)
www.drianbillinghurst.com

Dr. Richard Pitcairn/Animal Natural Health Center
(alternative veterinarian and author)
www.drpitcairn.com

Haggerty's School for Dogs, Inc.
www.HaggertyDog.com

Holistic Healing
www.holisticmed.com/www/veterinary.html

Miriam Fields-Babineau (manufacturer of the Comfort Trainer)
www.miriamfields.com

United Kennel Club
   www.ukcdogs.com

Woman's Best Friend Community
   www.womansbestfriend.org

DOG-TRAINING ORGANIZATIONS

Before hiring any trainer, do your homework. Observe classes, shop around, and go with your gut. Qualifications for memberships in these organizations range from simply paying a membership fee to taking an exam and being sponsored. Each organization has a different purpose. Visit the websites for more information.

Association of Pet Dog Trainers (APDT)
   www.apdt.com

International Association of Canine Professionals (IACP)
   www.dogpro.org

National Association of Dog Obedience Instructors (NADOI)
   www.nadoi.org

Index